CLASSIC
CHRISTIANITY

BOB GEORGE

HARVEST HOUSE PUBLISHERS
EUGENE, OREGON

Cover by Dugan Design Group, Bloomington, Minnesota

CLASSIC CHRISTIANITY
Copyright © 1989 by Harvest House Publishers
Eugene, Oregon 97402
www.harvesthousepublishers.com

ISBN 978-0-7369-2673-7 (pbk.)
ISBN 978-0-7369-3948-5 (eBook)

Library of Congress Cataloging-in-Publication data
  George, Bob, 1933–
  Classic Christianity.
  Includes bibliographical references.
  1. Christian life—1960– . 2. George, Bob, 1933– . I. Title.
  BV4501.2.G42 1989 248.4 87-83230
  ISBN 978-0-89081-660-8

Printed in the United States of America

15 16 / VP-SK / 10 9 8

CONTENTS

⤳

A Word from the Publisher

BY BOB HAWKINS JR.,
PRESIDENT OF HARVEST HOUSE PUBLISHERS

I recall that sunny afternoon around 1986 as if it were yesterday. While driving down Hilyard Street in Eugene, Oregon, I tuned in to a local Christian radio station in search of a solid sermon from a well-known preacher. Instead, I found myself captivated by a biblical counseling call-in program—an unusual broadcast for a time when teachings like "Christian psychology" and "improving your self-esteem" dominated the airwaves.

The compassion of the teacher and the biblical focus of the counsel drew me to listen all the more. And I was pleased when I heard that the counselor and his ministry were located in Dallas, Texas, a city I would soon be visiting on business. So I scheduled an appointment to meet with the host of the program, Bob George of People to People Ministries, hoping to provide their outreach with some appropriate Harvest House books as premiums for their broadcast.

Bob will tell you more about the misunderstanding that followed, but the upshot was, he talked for nearly two hours at the appointment about who we are in Christ and the problems with today's performance-based Christianity. I was riveted! I found myself nodding in wholehearted agreement with what made complete sense from my personal study of God's Word. My past reading of the Bible was being illuminated with fresh insight right there on the spot. I had not heard such freeing news in my entire Christian life!

I had grown up in a strong Christian environment, and my constant heart's desire was to better understand how to grow in my walk with the

Lord. However, like so many of you who have opened these pages, I found myself struggling to keep sin at bay while striving to live the Christian life out of my own strength. I had a good handle on the basic doctrines of the Bible, and I was convinced Christ had died for and forgiven all my sins. After all, I was living *for* Christ. Yet something was missing amid all my efforts. I was "busy and barren," as Bob George puts it. But I was about to embark on an amazing journey of biblical understanding, just as you are now.

That two-hour discussion in Dallas led to the first publication of *Classic Christianity*, in 1989. The book's impact has far exceeded the expectations of both author and publisher—over 600,000 copies have been distributed worldwide in numerous languages! And the stories keep coming in about people transformed by the love and grace of Christ. In fact, I would go so far as to say that *Classic Christianity* represents the purest presentation of the gospel message I have ever read. Why? Because it effectively strips away, to the degree mere man can, all but "Christ, who is your life" (Colossians 3:4).

Finally, as president of Harvest House Publishers, I want to express my deep appreciation to and love for Bob and Amy George, Bob and Jeanna Christopher, Bob Davis, and so many other truly ministry-minded servants at People to People Ministries. These 20 years have been a huge joy for my wife and me and our staff! Thank you for welcoming Harvest House as an integral partner in your life-changing outreach.

And to you, the reader, if you want to understand who you are in Christ, if you want to stop striving and start resting, if you want to truly grow in your Christian life, read this book in its entirety, again and again. (And don't miss the foreword by Major Ian Thomas, which alone is worth the price of the book!)

With eternal appreciation to God the Father and His servant Bob George,

Bob Hawkins Jr.
President, Harvest House Publishers

FOREWORD

BY MAJOR IAN THOMAS

There are few things quite so boring as being religious, but there is nothing quite so exciting as being a Christian!

Most folks have never discovered the difference between the one and the other, so that there are those who sincerely try to live a life they do not have, substituting religion for God, Christianity for Christ, and their own noble endeavors for the energy, joy, and power of the Holy Spirit. In the absence of reality, they can only grasp at ritual, stubbornly defending the latter in the absence of the former, lest they be found with neither!

They are lamps without oil, cars without gas, and pens without ink, baffled at their own impotence in the absence of all that alone can make man functional; for man was so engineered by God that the presence of the Creator within the creature is indispensable to his humanity. Christ gave Himself *for* us to give Himself *to* us! His presence puts God back into the man! He came that we might have life—God's life!

There are those who have a life they never live. They have come to Christ and thanked Him only for what He did, but do not live in the power of who He is. Between the Jesus who "was" and the Jesus who "will be" they live in a spiritual vacuum, trying with no little zeal to live for Christ a life that only He can live in and through them, perpetually begging for what in Him they already have!

It is to those who try to live a life they do not have, and to those who have a life they do not live that Bob George addresses himself in these

7

pages, vividly illustrated out of his own personal experience and that of those with whom he has counseled. Here is the truth that sets men free. This is where "the rubber hits the road," a book full of spiritual insight and common sense, enjoyable and easy-to-read. I am convinced that many, heartily sick of the "rat race," will in reading these pages find in the Lord Jesus Christ the final answer to their need.

—Major W. Ian Thomas
Torchbearers of the
Capernwray Missionary
Fellowship

IT'S ALL FROM HIM

The story of *Classic Christianity* is truly miraculous. Since its initial release in 1989, I have seen God use this book in ways I could never have planned, dreamed, or even remotely imagined. Even the way the book came into existence is miraculous.

For years, the staff members of People to People Ministries and I had talked about the need to write a book. We had seen and experienced how the truths of God's love and grace had changed our lives. And we were seeing how the fullness of the gospel was making a difference in other people's lives as we spoke these truths on our radio broadcast, *People to People*. So the desire grew in my heart to one day write down a description of my journey to discover the grace of God. However, with a schedule filled to overflowing, we hardly had time to even *think* about a book. But we continued to talk about the need, and "we've got to get a book out" almost became the ministry byline.

Around 1986, Bob Hawkins Jr., at that time vice president of marketing for Harvest House Publishers, dropped by our office to discuss the possibility of advertising some of their books on our radio program. When he arrived, one of our staff escorted him back to my office and said, "Bob Hawkins, vice president of Harvest House, is here to talk about…" And I understood him to say "a book."

Delighted, I thought, *Lord, thank You for this opportunity. This must finally be the time to write that book.* So I proceeded to describe the book we wanted to produce. I kept wondering why Bob had such a puzzled look on his face as I went on with my presentation. But he sat patiently and heard me out. And after I had finished, he looked straight at me and declared, "I didn't come here to talk about a book, but after hearing what you've said, that is a book we are going to publish!"

We never envisioned that one day *Classic Christianity* would be translated into 26 foreign languages. Nor did we even imagine it would sell over 600,000 copies worldwide. In fact, when Bob told me the initial printing was going to be 5000 copies, I wondered how many of those we were going to have to "eat" ourselves.

It says a lot about *Classic Christianity* that it "goes out the door" in quantity. For example, every month a doctor in El Paso buys a case to give out to his patients. A bus driver we know passes them out to his passengers free of charge. These kinds of things would never take place unless people were having their lives changed by the message. Those who know Christ Jesus and are experiencing His love and grace can't help but share it with others.

It fascinates me that the life of this book has taken on a worldwide scope. The gospel of Jesus Christ knows no cultural boundaries, and *Classic Christianity*'s spread abroad is another testimony to the fact. It makes no difference whether you're proclaiming the pure gospel in Indonesia or in Indiana—the response is the same. Since people the world over are searching for truth, when they find it in the person of Jesus Christ, their lives *change*.

The nation of Russia is one place where this truth has started to take root. My wife, Amy, was born in Russia (she tells the amazing story of her journey to America in *Goodbye Is Not Forever*). Over the years, we have both had a strong desire to share our message in her homeland, but we've had no idea how to make this happen. So we basically, said, "Lord, if this is going to come about, You're going to have to do it." And He *did* do it—in a way that we could never have dreamed of—through a young man named Dmitri Romanov.

In the 1980s, while Dmitri was in the Russian army, somebody shared the gospel with him. He gave his heart to the Lord but did not experience much growth. After his service in the army, Dmitri returned to his hometown of Kazan. He did not own a Bible, and during the

Cold War the only way to get one was through the black market—but Dmitri did not have the money. However, when he discovered that an elderly lady living in the same apartment building had a Bible, he borrowed it from her. Over the next 40 days he hand-copied the *entire New Testament.*

Dmitri was very eager to learn, but most of the teaching he encountered was very legalistic and controlling. The state-approved religious groups he affiliated himself with taught him that a great gap existed between him and God, and the only way to close that gap was through good works. So in his zeal he dedicated his whole life to doing good things, trying to get closer to God.

"Every person in our part of the world needs to read this book. I am going to translate *Classic Christianity* into Russian."

When Communism fell in Russia, the windows of opportunity opened for the spread of Christianity. A group of Christians in Donetsk, Ukraine, gathered what resources they could to start a Bible college. But the college needed an administrator, so one of the leaders who had known Dmitri called him to see if he would take the position. To Dmitri this was a great opportunity to shorten the gap between him and God. "This will increase my 'karma,'" was his thought, as he later told me. "If God is pleased with me now, just think how pleased He will be with me as the administrator of a Bible college." So he took the job.

While this was taking place in Russia, a widower in his sixties named George, an avid listener to our *People to People* radio broadcast in St. Louis, Missouri, was looking for a new wife and companion. For some reason he was interested in finding a *Russian* wife. He placed personal ads describing his aim in several Russian newspapers, asking that any woman who responded also send a picture. Needless to say, he received hundreds of replies.

But George wasn't interested in just any Russian woman—he wanted to find a *Christian* Russian woman. To those women whose pictures he found attractive, he sent a copy of *Classic Christianity.* One woman in particular who piqued his interest was from Donetsk, Ukraine. They wrote several letters back and forth; of course, each time they needed someone to translate the letters so they could understand what had been written.

It wasn't long before George decided to travel to Ukraine. And one day he just showed up on this woman's doorstep to see her and figure out whether she was truly the one he wanted to marry. He couldn't understand Russian, and she couldn't understand English! But she had a friend who could speak both. His name was—Dmitri Romanov.

Dmitri and his wife, Gulya, who was also fluent in English, came over to interpret. During their conversation, George perceived that Dmitri was steeped in legalism. "This guy needs help," he said to himself, and he gave Dmitri a copy of *Classic Christianity*.

Dmitri did not put the book down until he had finished it. That night the grace of God captured his heart and changed his life. The next day he excitedly told George, "Every person in our part of the world needs to read this book. I am going to translate *Classic Christianity* into Russian."

As a result of that encounter, over 75,000 copies of *Classic Christianity* have been published in Russian and distributed. Almost daily we receive letters from people throughout that part of the world, sharing how the book has opened their understanding to the truths of God's love and grace.

How did all this happen? I can tell you, it sure wasn't the result of my planning, or of our staff meeting together to hammer out strategies to reach global markets. It is all God, and He is the one to whom all the praise and glory belongs.

He saw a guy in Russia trying to increase his "karma." He saw another man in St. Louis looking for a wife—and He said, "I can use that." God is the only one with the big picture. He is the only one who can take the common—or the slightly uncommon—events of life and use them for His glory.

Another fascinating story of the spread of the gospel involves my good friend Tom Grady, the president of Grace Ministries in Atlanta, Georgia. Several years ago he established an office in Budapest, Hungary, for the purpose of training leaders for various ministries—including YWAM (Youth With A Mission). As part of their work, YWAM trains and then sends out missionary teams all over Eastern Europe. After Tom introduced their leadership to *Classic Christianity,* the book made such a tremendous impact that believers have translated it into every language of the Balkan states for use in their missionary efforts.

And *Classic Christianity* has also been translated into Chinese. A professor at the University of Texas, Charlie Chew, attended a seminar we hosted. At that seminar he got a copy of the book. It so deeply touched his life that, as so many others have done, he passed it on—in this case to his sister and brother-in-law. They read it and immediately decided it needed to be translated into Chinese. They wanted to take the book into mainland China to help the Christians there see and understand the freedom that is available to them in Christ Jesus. Today, every time they travel to China, they carry with them Chinese Bibles and Chinese translations of *Classic Christianity* to help them share the good news of Jesus Christ.

These are just a few of the miraculous stories I could tell you about the spread of the good news. How God works in marvelous, miraculous ways! He is truly a wondrous God, who has promised to complete the good work He has begun in us (Philippians 1:6). When I realized the truth of this promise many years ago, my life totally changed. And the older I get and the longer I am in the Lord, the more I see that it is all of *Him* and none of me.

~

When this book was first released in 1989, my desire was that God would use it to call people back to "Classic Christianity." I'm sure you can already see that I believe God has answered that prayer over these past 20 years.

In addition to the miraculous stories I've already told, *Classic Christianity* has found its way into the hands of world leaders, Christian missionaries, churches, pastors, and ministry leaders. Copies are circulating behind prison walls, are being passed around entire congregations, and are finding their way to individuals who are burned out and bogged down by religion.

When I was driving to the busiest Christian schedule you could imagine, crying out to God to take me back to the days when I first knew

Him, I thought I was the only one feeling this spiritual unrest. What I discovered when I began to share my journey was that my story was not unique. That same cry reverberates within the hearts of Christians all over the world. People are longing for answers, truths that can change the course of their lives and bring peace to their hearts.

Classic Christianity addresses that spiritual unrest and calls people back to the liberating truths of the gospel of Jesus Christ. For 20 years, God has used this book to deliver people who are bound up into the freedom of God's love and grace, and to show those who are merely going through the motions the way to experience true abundant life in Christ Jesus.

In his final years, the apostle Paul expressed his sole desire in life:

> If only I may finish the race and complete the task the Lord Jesus has given me—the task of testifying to the gospel of God's grace (Acts 20:24).

I believe all of us who name the name of Christ are called to testify to God's grace. It is the one message that matters. It is the one message that changes lives.

Thousands of people have written letters to tell me how the grace of God has changed their lives. These have been a real source of encouragement and have given me even greater resolve to carry on with the task at hand. I am honored to share some of the most meaningful ones with you.

> *"I was really a depressed person. Even though I was a Christian, my life was still in constant turmoil. I was even contemplating suicide. I found your radio program, and you gave me hope. I ordered* Classic Christianity. *Your book made a huge difference in my life. I found real purpose and hope, real life in Jesus Christ."*
>
> —RAY, ARIZONA

> *"When I went to prison, I carried a heavy burden not knowing whether God had given up on me or not. It became very important for me to find this out. I got a copy of* Classic Christianity, *read it and reread it probably more than 100 times in the next three years. I don't know how many lives you have changed over the last*

30 years, but I do know that God used you to change one life on the other side of the world."

—Warren, Brisbane, Australia

"About ten years ago I was struggling, wondering why Christianity doesn't work…why I was feeling as empty as a believer as I did when I was an unbeliever. A friend suggested that my wife and I read Classic Christianity. *The gospel of God's grace and peace took hold of our lives. Life is still challenging, but underneath all the daily problems and puzzles is a bedrock, which is Christ and not us."*

—Kermit, Wisconsin

"My friend had given me a copy of Classic Christianity *to give to my brother. I was struggling at the time with guilt, frustration, and anger. Guilt over past sins, anger because I couldn't understand why trying to live the Christian life was impossible, and frustrated over it all. I told God that I was giving up on Christianity. Then I remembered the book my friend had given me. Recalling the subtitle I thought, 'Life is too short to miss the real thing. Well, I'm missing it so I'd better read this book.'*

"I could not put it down. I felt the scales falling off my eyes. I began to see life and God's love in a whole new way—His way. Wow, He loved me first. What a concept! It has been a tremendous journey, and to this day I just have faith in God through Jesus that He will finish His work in me—it truly is an exciting life. God used your book in a tremendous way that is impacting everyone around my family. I have your book in my office in English and Spanish to give away to my clients."

—Valoree, California

"I could not put Classic Christianity *down. I took two days to go to my ranch with it and my Bible. If you were wrong, I would know it. If you were right, I was going to shout it from the rooftops. As God opened my heart and my eyes to understand the New Covenant and my identity in Christ, my life, my family, and my ministry*

were transformed. I have had the opportunity of sharing that message with thousands. The impact of Christ through you continues through the many lives you have touched, including mine."

—BILL, TEXAS

God is calling people back to the simplicity of the gospel…back to His grace, mercy, and truth…back to the person of Jesus Christ. Respond to His call, and experience the freedom that is yours in Him.

—Bob George
People to People Ministries
Dallas, Texas, 2009

CLASSIC
CHRISTIANITY

1

BUSY AND BARREN

It was another Monday morning, and I was inching along Central Expressway toward downtown Dallas and the busiest schedule you can imagine. Once again, my eyes clouded with tears as I sat immobile in the snarled traffic. Why was I so miserable? Why were tears becoming an almost daily experience?

What made this condition all the more perplexing was that I was already doing all the "right things" the Christian world said I should. I studied the Bible extensively, memorized hundreds of Scriptures, witnessed to everybody I met, and prayed constantly. My church commitment was total—I was there Sunday morning, Sunday night, Monday night for visitation, Wednesday night, plus other times for innumerable committee meetings. There wasn't much more I could do in church.

But that's just the beginning. I was also in full-time Christian service, with the emphasis on "full-time." I was teaching in a Bible college and serving as minister of evangelism for one of the largest churches in America, while at the same time serving as president of a ministry which I had founded. I was writing Bible-study books, doing a daily 15-minute radio broadcast, and teaching seminars all over Dallas and around the country. Busy? You better believe it!

My frustration had nothing to do with a desire for the world's goods. I had tried all that long ago in the business world. For all of my adult life to the age of 36, I worked to become a millionaire, seeking meaning and purpose to life in things. But that didn't bring satisfaction. I then became the owner of my own thriving business, thinking that what I needed was to be my own boss. But that didn't change anything either. I socialized and even hobnobbed with Hollywood celebrities. But I found that they were just as empty as I was. I called it a life of "cars, bars, and movie stars." But I still wasn't happy or fulfilled.

> My Christian life had been vibrant, alive, thrilling. Now it was tied up worse than this freeway traffic.

Then, through a dramatic series of events, I learned that Jesus Christ had died for my sins and was raised again so that I might experience God's forgiveness and new life in Him. At that moment, I turned my life over to Christ. I prayed, "Lord Jesus, if You can change me, come into me and do it. I sure need to be changed."

And He did! For the first time in my life, I discovered what it was to experience love. God took a marriage that was headed for the rocks and put us back together. I learned for the first time the joys of being a father—I had always been too busy before. No longer was I wrapped up in myself in a headlong drive for success. I became more concerned with giving other people the greatest message ever known to man and introducing people to the same Lord Jesus who had changed my life. Each day became a thrilling adventure. I had never been happier.

But that had been eight years ago. What happened?

The tears only intensified, flowing freely down my cheeks as I reviewed my life. I thought again of the words to a song by Andraé Crouch: "Lord, take me back to the days when I first knew You." My heart was crying out to God as I softly sang the song to myself.

It didn't make an ounce of sense. A few years earlier, my Christian life had been vibrant, alive, thrilling. Now it was tied up worse than this freeway traffic, bogged down and barely inching along. Where had I gone wrong?

~⁂~

Today, I realize my experience was not unique. As I talk with Christians all over the country, I hear them asking, "What's wrong?" Many of them are doing all the "right things," just as I did. Yet they feel like they're racing madly on a spiritual treadmill. They're highly active, but going nowhere.

Many go from seminar to seminar, Web site to Web site, book to book, desperately trying to find the missing link that will make the Christian life really work for them. Our generation has more Christian learning resources available than any generation in history. But I have to ask: Are we really better off? Are we more joyful? Are we more faithful? Do we have a deeper experience of God and His love?

It reminds me of a remark made to me by Major Ian Thomas:

> If an unbeliever were to walk into a Christian bookstore, he would see the shelves just blanketed with "how-to" books—everything from how to run a Christian business, to how to lead a Christian exercise class, to how to cook a Christian dinner. His response would probably be, "Don't you Christians know how to do *anything*?"

I have to agree with Major Thomas. I think we have strayed far from God's real priorities for us. With all our "how-to" resources, I believe we have forgotten how to *live*. We have forgotten that the Christian life is *Christ*, not just a change of lifestyle. But, straying from Christ Himself as our life, we have no other option than to substitute furious activity and service. It has gotten to the point where, to be a member of many churches today, you don't need to pass a doctrinal exam; you need to pass a physical! Sheer physical endurance has become more essential than spiritual enlightenment to assume a position in leadership.

God began to get my attention through an occasion that I will never forget. Mac, a hard-driving, tough businessman in his seventies, had been a church member for many years. But one Wednesday night as he heard me share my personal testimony, he realized that he had never personally trusted in Jesus Christ as his Savior. Though he had been involved in a lot of religious activity, he had never really had a clear idea of what it meant to be a Christian.

After spending a few days pondering and asking me questions, Mac made up his mind. At the Sunday night service of our church, he decided to come forward to make a public profession of his faith in Christ. I was down at the front serving as counselor, and I was deeply moved by the sight of this tough old businessman coming forward to receive Christ in childlike faith. We were both in tears as we stood before the pastor.

"Bob, this is tremendous!" the pastor exclaimed. "This man is one of the most brilliant businessmen in our city! He's wealthy, he's talented, and we need to put him to work! I want you to see that Mac is totally involved in what you're doing. We want to take full advantage of what he can do."

I will never forget Mac, his eyes full of tears, speaking with a sincere, trembling voice: *"Pastor, I don't need a job. I need the Lord."*

The instant I heard Mac's reply, I knew that he was speaking with greater wisdom than he could have been aware of. And I also thought to myself, "Maybe that's what is wrong with *me.*" My Christian life at the time did feel more like a job than a relationship.

On the Treadmill

I have heard the same sad admission from many other Christians, too. Someone experiences a genuine conversion to Jesus Christ that results in immediate changes. But there seems to be something lacking in knowing how to live from that point. He dutifully obeys the instructions that other believers give him, and jumps onto the treadmill of service. It isn't long before he discovers that no amount of service—sincere though it may be—will make a person spiritual. In desperation he redoubles his efforts but, like a person struggling in quicksand, it seems that the harder he tries, the deeper he sinks.

Other people get bound up in fear and guilt, effectively frustrating their personal growth. Mary, for example, wrote to me about her experiences:

> I was brought up in a strict denomination where I learned to be afraid of God. I've gone to many churches since becoming a born-again Christian, talked with many pastors, have been sent to many doctors, counselors, psychiatrists, psychologists. You name it, I've been there. But it wasn't until I started learning of God's grace and total forgiveness that I started to become free...Now I am no longer carrying the burden of sin on my

back, constantly looking over my shoulder to see if God is running after me with His great big wooden spoon.

I have learned that this experience Mary describes is shared by many other believers. Like children living under hyperauthoritarian parents, they live in a state of constant worry that they will suffer the application of God's big wooden spoon. Consciously or unconsciously, they live by a list of rules. When they keep those rules, they are "okay." When they slip, they get ready to bend over. As a result, many born-again Christians live in terrible bondage, constantly worrying if they are obeying the right rules or doing the right activities to please God. An oppressive burden of guilt becomes their normal, everyday experience.

We don't necessarily recognize these people as hurting. On the outside, they may be smiling, repeating the usual Christian clichés, and performing the expected church functions. But inside, they know they are putting on an act. They would love to be free of the burden. They deeply desire to share their fears, pains, and doubts, but don't for fear of being condemned. So they suffer their own silent condemnation, wondering if God will ever find it in His heart to accept them.

Just recently while teaching a Bible study series on dealing with fear and anxiety, I asked the class to write down their answers to this question: "What are you afraid of?" Among the many predictable responses were a few that were heartbreaking. One man described his greatest anxiety as "The fear of not getting right with the Lord and continuing to live a lie." After many years of being a personal counselor, I can tell you that this anonymous writer is not alone.

"That's Just the Way It Is"

Is this, then, what Jesus had in mind when He talked of an "abundant life"? No! But if people have never experienced anything different, they will accept their predicament as normal. They will assume "that's just the way it is."

A vivid example comes from the childhood of my wife, Amy, who grew up in Ukraine during the famine-stricken years of the 1930s. Amy never had a pair of shoes until she was eight years old. Then one exciting day someone came up with a pair of old, used shoes that they thought she might be able to wear. She crinkled up her little toes to get her feet into those shoes, which were too small for her. "How do they fit?" her mother asked.

"They fit great!" exclaimed little Amy with a big grin. She was so thankful to have any shoes at all—plus, having no previous experience, she had nothing to compare them to. So she said thank you and ran off to play. For a long time afterward, Amy's definition of the word *shoes* would have been something like this: "They're those things that make your feet hurt, but enable you to go outside and play in cold weather."

Then the day came when she finally tried on a pair of shoes of the proper size. Amazing! They didn't hurt anymore. It dawned on her that what she had always accepted as normal was not normal at all—that shoes could be made to fit and to make your feet feel better.

I believe this story illustrates the lives of many Christians. Obviously, knowing that we are going to heaven when we die is better than uncertainty and the fear of judgment. But we have come to expect very little from the Christian life down here on earth. We settle for being a sort of "second-class Christian."

When you are hearing all about what you *ought* to be experiencing but aren't, you feel trapped between two choices: Either admit the truth and be embarrassed or put up a front and pretend you are doing great.

If you have ever felt caught in this dilemma, I have got great news. The Christian life really *isn't* a matter of perfecting your acting ability. It *can* be real! I know your hurts, because I have been there. But in this book I'm going to share with you the truths that God has used in my life to set me free. It took me several years to learn these things. Much of what I now know, I learned the hard way—through personal failure. But those lessons are often the ones that are most valuable over a lifetime.

Starting Out Toward Freedom

It was that very day while I sat stranded on a jammed freeway that God began to lead me to the answers I was looking for. I remembered a statement that Jesus made: "You will know the truth, and the truth will make you free" (John 8:32 NASB). It occurred to me that if "truth sets you free," the opposite also had to be true: Error puts you in bondage.

Identifying this principle was a significant turning point for me. *Truth sets you free; error binds you.*

My keen mind quickly identified the fact that I was certainly not free! There could be only one reason why: I was living according to error rather than according to truth. Therefore my next thought was to ask the obvious question: "In what areas have I fallen into error in my Christian life?" I thought back to those early days of knowing the Lord, when I was fresh and eager, and compared them to my present experience. In many areas, there was a sharp contrast.

Religion vs. the Son

Some of the issues involved were things as fundamental as my approach to Bible study. When I received Christ at the age of 36, I immersed myself aggressively in the Bible. For several months, my wife thought I had a black-leather face! I was always in the Word. But over time, my sincere love of Christ became overshadowed by my increasing theological knowledge.

In my preoccupation with God's Word (which was certainly good in its initial form), I failed to see something. Jesus never said the Word would set us free. It's the *truth* of the Word that sets us free. Jesus said, "If you continue in My word...you will know the *truth*, and the *truth* will make you free" (John 8:31-32 NASB). He went on to say, "So if the *Son* sets you free, you will be free indeed" (John 8:36). Where does the truth of the Word lead you? To the Son!

I knew the Bible frontward and backward, but that knowledge alone didn't change my condition. In my experience, Jesus got lost in the Bible. I remembered how He had said to the Pharisees,

> You diligently study the Scriptures because you think that by them you possess eternal life. These are the Scriptures that testify about *Me, yet you refuse to come to Me* to have life (John 5:39-40).

I remembered a phrase that was very popular in evangelistic appeals. It was the answer to a common non-Christian comment—"I don't like religion." The comeback is, "Christianity is not a religion; it's a *relationship* with God through His Son, Jesus Christ." That phrase is absolutely true. But I saw with amazement that, while I continued to quote it in situations where I was sharing Christ with an unbeliever, in my own life I had strayed from my relationship with God back to practicing a religion!

I longed for the joy I had experienced during the first two years of my Christian life. In those days, I often awoke at 4:00 in the morning—and I'm not generally an early riser—to pick up the Bible and enjoy an intimate time with my heavenly Father. No one told me to do that. I *wanted* to do it.

During those first two years as a Christian it was a joy just to be alive. For the first time, I was discovering what it meant to really love my family. I spoke to business groups about my faith. I taught Bible studies. I would make a $20,000 sale in my business, but be more excited about the chance to tell the customer about Jesus.

Working for God

What a contrast to my frequent tears on the Dallas freeway during rush hour just a few years later. What had gone wrong? It seemed that the excitement started to slip away after I sold my business and went into "full-time" Christian work. It was obvious that my heart was no longer in business, and what could be better than doing full-time what I enjoyed doing as a businessman? I thought I had attained the ultimate—a life totally dedicated to the ministry.

> When you have lost the joy of your salvation and have begun sharing Christ out of habit, competition, or just plain duty…what can you say? "Become a Christian and be miserable like me"?

But somehow it was never quite what I expected. I still taught Bible studies. I still shared my faith. But it became more of a performance. Instead of doing it because I wanted to, I did it because I was expected to do it. Someone reminded me to make sure and have a "quiet time" in the morning. I had to fill out reports indicating how many people I shared Christ with and how many Bible studies I was leading. My joy ebbed away, and those activities became more mechanical. The early-morning times with the Lord that I enjoyed so much became less and less frequent as other things began demanding my attention. After having led hundreds of people to Christ as a businessman, I found myself losing interest in talking to people about the Lord. Don't get me wrong; I still experienced a tremendous thrill when someone was born again. But when you have lost the joy of your salvation and have begun sharing Christ out of habit, competition, or just plain duty, there is no relish in it and not much to keep you going. After all, what can you say? "Become a Christian and be miserable like me"?

I thought of the challenge that initially had drawn me to full-time ministry: "Come Help Change the World." I had responded to the challenge and jumped in to help change the world. But I don't think the world changed much.

After a couple years of service in Southern California, I was sent to Dallas to head up a major, citywide evangelistic campaign. For three years, I poured my life into that cause—to help change Dallas. But when the campaign was over, I had to admit that Dallas really hadn't changed.

After considerable evaluation, I decided that what was really needed was a ministry to help change the church from within. I started training leaders who would in turn train other leaders in the local church. I became director of evangelism for one of the world's largest churches. But soon it became obvious that I couldn't change the church. In fact, it was becoming more and more ludicrous to think about changing anything around me *when I couldn't even change me*. If I couldn't change me, how could I possibly think I was going to change the world?

That was another error that was binding me. As I thought about it, I finally realized that *Christ didn't call me to change anything; He called me to proclaim the truth!* It's no wonder I was frustrated. I was pursuing a goal that God never gave me. In that pursuit of a goal God never gave me, I had absolutely lost the joy of knowing Him. What was once the overflow of my experience of God's love had become just an external performance. I was totally committed to God's *plan*, true—but I had strayed away from the *God* of the plan. I could deny it for a while, but I wanted reality too much to keep up a pretense for long, even with Christians applauding, patting me on the back, and telling me how well I was doing.

Well, I was tired of it. Just plain sick and tired of being sick and tired. I wanted to experience again the joy of my salvation. As I pulled off the freeway and drew near to my office, I prayed a simple prayer:

Lord, I don't care what the organization that I used to be with taught me. I don't care what the church I'm in or the denomination to which I belong has taught me. I want *You* to teach me afresh, all over again. I want to know the truth that You promised would set me free. I'm tired of listening to people. I'm ready to listen to You.

⇌

Today, a number of years later, I can tell you that God is more real to me than I ever dreamed possible. I now enjoy genuine freedom through understanding who I am in Christ. My relationship with God is now even more exciting than when it first began in 1969. Ironically, I'm probably just as busy, or busier, than I was before. But the work of the ministry is no longer a burden; it's a joy! I'm no longer trying to change the world or anything else. I am content to let God work through me to produce whatever results He pleases.

In this book, I'm going to share with you what I learned.

If you have ever felt that your Christian life is more like a job than an adventure; or if you have ever found yourself saying, "There's got to be more to the Christian life than what I'm experiencing"; or if you are *not* a Christian, but a seeker who has been confused by the bewildering denominations and factions, who wonders if there is a "real thing" at all—I invite you to join me on a journey. It's the journey I took through the Scriptures and through real-life experiences. A journey to discover not just the *words* of the Bible. A journey to discover the *truth* of the words in the Bible. More than anything else, I wanted to know more fully the Person of Jesus Christ whom the Bible reveals. I thank God with all my heart that He led me to find what I was looking for—a return to Classic Christianity. It's my prayer today that you, too, will discover *or rediscover* the real thing.

The passages we examine may be familiar to you. You may already know many of the verses by heart. What I hope and pray you find in this book is the *truth* of these verses that will set you free. I pray that your eyes will be opened and that you will see all the incredible gifts God has chosen to give to those who love Him.

2

THE TRUTH ABOUT ERROR

It had been nearly three years since I had talked to Pete. He was an alcoholic whom I had tried to counsel for a while. But Pete wouldn't take responsibility for his problem and finally stopped seeing me. So I was surprised one night to get a phone call from him.

It wasn't a very pleasant conversation. He asked a favor of me that I was unable to fulfill, to which he responded with a long string of profanity. "Pete, you're using that language to shock me," I said, remaining calm. "But it won't work. At one time I probably used it more than you."

"I hate you!" he responded.

"Pete, that's your choice. But I love you."

That made him even madder. It's no fun to hate someone when that person won't hate you back. Finally he sputtered, "I'm going to get you!" and hung up.

I'm normally a pretty easygoing person, so this phone call didn't disturb me. I told Amy, my wife, about it and expressed to her how sad it was that Pete wouldn't recognize the truth and enter into the freedom that Christ wanted to provide him. It was late, so we headed to bed. About 15 minutes after we had turned out the lights, I heard a car screech into our driveway. I got up and looked out the window. The car door opened and out stepped a wild-eyed man with unkempt, bushy hair, holding a long butcher knife. It was Pete!

My heart jumped up into my throat. "Amy, get in the closet!" I yelled. Quickly, I ran into my son's room, ordered him under the bed, and grabbed a baseball bat out of his closet. I ran past my daughter's room and told her to hide under her bed. I stopped in the foyer by the front door and waited. I could feel my heart racing and my ears straining to hear any noise.

For a moment, I was tempted to relax, knowing the front door was locked. Then I heard a loud thump as the man put all of his 200 pounds into a brutal kick. Another kick followed, and the door flew open. Instantly the man sprang into the house. But I was waiting for him. With all of my strength, I sent the baseball bat crashing down onto his head. Blood spattered against the wall as he crumpled. But I didn't let up. I hit him again and again until I was sure he was unconscious.

Then I backed away, horrified at what I had done. I turned and ran into the kitchen and called the police...

And all of this took place that very night—*in my mind*—while I was lying in my nice, warm bed.

∼≥∽

The phone call from Pete actually occurred. The rest was only my overactive imagination taking Pete's words "I'm going to get you!" and living out the possibilities that soon seemed only too real. Pete never came to my house. There was nothing to fear. Yet my heart was pounding, and my body was sweating and trembling with anger as I thought about defending my family.

I experienced these things because of a basic fact about human beings: Our emotions can't distinguish between fact and fantasy. My emotions didn't know that there was no real danger. They simply responded to the messages sent by my brain. It was as if the events I described were really happening. That's the danger with error. Whatever we put into our minds will affect our emotions.

Our emotions always follow our thoughts. They are responders. If you don't believe it, go to a theater and watch a scary movie. Years ago I went to see Alfred Hitchcock's *Psycho*. I remember sitting in the theater, eating popcorn, aware of the light from the film projector above my head, and being scared out of my socks at what I was seeing on the screen. I'm sure you have had the same experience.

Now think about it—isn't that ridiculous? There was absolutely no danger to me; it was just a movie. But my emotions didn't know that—they thought it was real. They were responding predictably to the messages being sent through my "eye gate" and "ear gate." That's the way we are made. Whatever a man puts into his mind and *thinks* about determines what he will *feel*.

The Power of Error-Controlled Thinking

We can't control our emotions. We can only control our thoughts. There is a phrase used by computer programmers that is represented by the initials GIGO. It means "garbage in, garbage out." Of course, the opposite is also true. True, realistic thoughts will produce realistic emotions. That is why the Bible is continually appealing to our *minds*, not our emotions. For example, Paul wrote in Philippians 4:8, "Finally, brothers, whatever is true, whatever is noble, whatever is right, whatever is pure, whatever is lovely, whatever is admirable—if anything is excellent or praiseworthy—*think about such things*." The thoughts we consistently feed into our minds will determine our emotions and desires, which will in turn determine our actions.

Man is free to put whatever he wants into his mind. His emotions will respond accordingly. If I am afraid, it is because I am thinking fearful thoughts. If I am angry, it's because I am thinking angry thoughts. If I am jealous, it's because I am thinking jealous thoughts.

Therefore, it is absolutely critical that we think thoughts that are truth rather than thoughts that are error. Further, it becomes essential that we learn to live as Christ taught us—one day at a time. Constantly reviewing the past once we have learned its lessons does nothing but stir up old emotions. Projecting into the future likewise raises emotions that can paralyze in the present. In fact, that's why many of our hospital beds are filled: Many psychiatric patients have lost their ability to cope with the present because of the error of becoming obsessed with either the past or the future.

A Case of Depression

One of the more graphic illustrations of the power of thinking error instead of truth and how it affects the emotions is the experience of Doreen. Ralph and Doreen had been friends of our family for several years. They were an outspoken Christian couple, heavily involved in their church. They also were active socially—members of the country club, participants in major fund-raising events in Dallas. Their children were grown and involved either in college or the start of their careers. By all outward appearances, this family had attained the good life.

But we all know that appearances can be deceiving. I didn't realize there was any serious problem until one day a friend of mine, who is an outstanding Dallas physician, called me to say that our mutual friend Doreen had just been admitted to Baylor Hospital in a fetal position. She had not washed her hair, bathed herself, or eaten a meal in days. She was being fed intravenously and was in such a state of depression that doctors had decided to send her over to the psychiatric ward the next day.

> My job was to identify the error that was in her mind and dispel it with the truth of God and His Word.

"Ralph is adamant. He does not want his wife undergoing psychiatric treatment," the doctor explained. "But I don't see any other option. However, Ralph has asked me to call you to see if you could go and talk to Doreen. Frankly, I don't think you can do any good, but I don't suppose it can hurt, either. Will you come and talk to her?"

Naturally, I agreed. As I drove over to the medical center, it was with the assurance that Jesus meant what He said in John 8:31-32—"If you hold to My teaching, you are really My disciples. Then you will know the truth, and the truth will set you free." Obviously Doreen was in bondage—in the fetal position, unable to feed or clean herself. According to Jesus, the reason she was in bondage was because of error. My job was to identify the error that was in her mind and dispel it with the truth of God and His Word.

In her private hospital room, I began by asking Doreen what was causing her problem. "What are you thinking about?" I asked. "What is going on in your life to cause you to get this depressed?"

"My daughter's getting married," Doreen began. "We've had nothing but problems since she announced her engagement. This man just isn't right for her. I've told her and told her, and she just won't listen. And then…" Doreen proceeded to explain that her daughter, Robin, didn't want a big wedding, but a small one. She wanted the reception at the country club rather than the church, and she wanted to serve champagne. Doreen had always envisioned throwing a big church wedding for Robin and, according to their denomination's beliefs, she didn't want champagne at the reception. "Now, after all the trouble we've gone to, Robin doesn't even want to have a church wedding. She's left home and moved to Oklahoma where her boyfriend lives."

"Well, that ought to be enough to drive anyone crazy," I said after she had completed her grim recital. "Let's break this down point by point, starting with the wedding," I said. "Whose wedding is it? Yours or your daughter's?"

"Robin's," she answered.

"Okay. Now Doreen, do you know the Lord Jesus Christ?"

"Yes."

"Then who lives in you?"

"Christ."

"And how about your daughter, Robin. Does she know Christ?"

"Yes, she does."

"And how about her fiancé?"

"Yes, he's a Christian."

"So all three of you are Christians. You all have Jesus Christ living in you. Yet you're not getting along at all. That doesn't make much sense, does it? Let me ask you, what is it about this man that you are so worried about? He knows the Lord. Robin loves him. What's the big worry? Why are you so upset over this man that Robin says is the man of her choice?" Doreen didn't answer my question, but started talking about the champagne issue. "Why do they insist on having champagne at the reception?"

"If they want to have champagne at the wedding, why not just let them have champagne at the wedding?" I countered. "If you don't want to buy it because of your convictions, then let them buy it. After all, it is their wedding."

"But the people from our church…it will be a scandal."

"So that's the problem. You're more interested in what the church people will think than what your daughter's desires are." Doreen winced at my words. I quickly pressed the issue. "Let me tell you this: After the wedding is over, the church people aren't going to be thinking about anything, and your daughter is going to be thinking about a lot. And what she's going to be thinking about is a mother and father who did not respect the kind of wedding she wanted to have. Not just the day after, but she'll be thinking about it for many, many years after. Forget about the other people! As I've said many times, 'If you're worried about what people are thinking about you—forget it; they're not!' Most of them will be thinking about themselves. That's just the way people are."

"Yes, but what about my daughter respecting my wishes?" Doreen protested. "She got angry at me. She's been disrespectful to me and her father—"

"Doreen, that may be true, but that's her responsibility. You can't control how she responds to you. You can only control how you respond to her."

"Yes, but…"

Our discussion continued in this vein for four hours. For every objection she raised, I attempted to expose the error and identify the truth. Finally, we got down to the bottom line. "Doreen, the fact of the matter is that you and Ralph have been acting like people who don't even know the Lord. You are paralyzed with fear, and you have self-righteousness and bitterness and hard feelings in your heart toward your daughter. What you are in essence saying is, 'Robin, I don't care what you want to do. You are going to have the kind of wedding we want you to have, not the kind you want.' Doreen, that is strictly selfishness. By doing this, you are going to lose your daughter, and all the details in the world about this wedding aren't worth losing your daughter."

Doreen wiped away her tears, and nodded in agreement. "My recommendation to you is to get on that phone right now and call Robin. You tell her you love her, and you tell her that if this is the man of *her* choice, then he's the man of *your* choice, and that you will take him into your family and love him just like you love her. And if she wants a small wedding, then we're going to have a small wedding. And if she wants to have a reception at the country club, we'll have a reception at the country club. It's her day. Do you agree with that?"

"Yes. I believe that's the right thing to do," she answered.

I stood up and moved toward the door as Doreen was dialing the phone. As I paused for a moment, I heard her say, "Robin, this is Mom. I love you. I'm sorry for the way we've been behaving. We've been acting like people that don't even know the Lord…" Soon she and her daughter were both crying over the phone as reconciliation was achieved. After she hung up, Doreen looked up at me and said, "The last thing Robin said was, 'Mom, I can't wait to get over and see you and Daddy.'"

Doreen was exhausted after our discussion, so I left to let her get some much-needed rest. Later that night the doctor called me at home and said, "Bob, what in the world did you do with Doreen?"

At first, the tone of his voice made me wonder if Doreen had relapsed or committed suicide or some other horror. So I answered, "I hope nothing. Why?"

He explained. "When I made my rounds tonight, Doreen was up. She'd bathed herself, fixed her hair, and eaten a huge meal. I'm releasing her from the hospital tomorrow morning."

Five years later, Doreen has a close relationship with her daughter and son-in-law. They had a wonderful wedding—the kind the daughter wanted. Everything turned out just fine.

Our Defense Against Error

So why was Doreen in the hospital, an emotional basket case? It wasn't because of reality. Rather, she was thinking about what things were going to be like based on her own preconceptions rather than on the actual facts. Frankly, that's the problem with most people who are severely depressed. They are not thinking about the truth. They are locked in error, and that error has them in emotional and physical bondage. Realizing, then, how important it is to be able to discern truth from error, how can we learn to tell the difference?

We might compare the problem to a banker who, knowing that there is counterfeit currency circulating, wants to teach his tellers how to distinguish between the real and the phony. The method he chooses is not to focus on counterfeits. Rather, he provides the tellers with so much exposure to real dollar bills that when a counterfeit bill slips in, it's obvious.

Likewise, Christians have one defense against error. That is to become so familiar with truth, as revealed by God in Scripture, that when they are confronted with error, it is easily discerned. But if Christians are not steeped in truth, they become gullible and vulnerable to all sorts of error.

The Lie

The war between truth and error has raged for thousands of years. When Adam and Eve sinned in the Garden of Eden, they didn't commit adultery. They didn't steal or break any of the other Ten Commandments. It all began when Adam and Eve believed a lie instead of the truth. God made only one decree to Adam, that he not eat of the tree of the knowledge of good and evil. Agreement with that one law meant Adam acknowledged that God and God alone determines what is right and wrong. The day Adam chose to eat of that tree, he became like God in the sense that he determined for himself right from wrong and good from evil. From the day of the fall, man has continued to say, in essence, "I know more than You, God, about what's right and wrong and good and evil. I don't need You to tell me the truth. I can discover it for myself." That's error, the ultimate error—the lie against the truth.

Today Satan's goal is, as it was in the garden, to convince us that the lie—the counterfeit—is actually the truth. We might illustrate it by imagining that you live near a beautiful, lush field. Let's suppose that one of your neighbors is secretly your enemy. He hates you, and is dedicated to hurting you. Your enemy knows that this beautiful piece of prime real estate is for sale, and that in addition to its aesthetic beauty, this land has oil underground. He cannot afford to purchase this land himself, but because he hates you so much, he is determined to do everything possible to prevent you from buying it. He accomplishes this for a time, but one day, when he is lax, you discover this land is for sale and buy it.

Your enemy is, of course, furious that you have bought the property, but he is powerless to change that fact. However, his hatred is so obsessive that he decides he will do everything possible to prevent you from ever learning that there is oil on the property. One strategy he employs is to keep you occupied with all kinds of activities—having potlucks and putting shuffleboard courts and other games on the land. He believes that if you are busy enough on the surface, you will never discover the oil that is underneath. If that doesn't work, he can try to divert you with all kinds of legal regulations and bureaucratic red tape that will bog you down and keep you from doing anything productive with the land. Whatever his methods, if he succeeds, your enemy will have done almost as much harm as if he had actually prevented you from buying the land in the first place.

> Satan was declawed and detoothed at the cross.
> All he can do is roar at us and gum us a little. The only way
> he can harm us is through deception.

That's exactly what Satan tries to do with us. Once we become children of God, able to plug into the truth, Satan has lost the most important battle. Now his only weapon against us is to try and fill our heads with error so that we never discover the incredible wealth that we have inherited as children of the living God. As we saw with Doreen, fear is one of his favorite tactics. Doreen was fearing the future. She had forgotten that "God did not give us a spirit of timidity [fear], but a spirit of power, of love and of self-discipline" (2 Timothy 1:7). Satan was declawed and detoothed at the cross. All he can do is roar at us and gum us a little. The only way he can harm us is through deception, through creating unfounded fears, through lies.

Opposing Lies with Truth

Satan will use any approach to keep us from experiencing the full measure of God's riches. Any error, no matter how small or great, will do. He works through the current world philosophies, through Bible verses taken out of context, through charismatic personalities who "sound" so right and sincere. No method is overlooked in Satan's attempt to mislead the chosen of God:

- Satan says: *Seek success at any price.* God says: "But seek first His kingdom and His righteousness, and all these things will be added to you" (Matthew 6:33 NASB).

- Satan says: *Seek riches at any cost.* God says: "Do not store up for yourselves treasures on earth...But store up for yourselves treasures in heaven" (Matthew 6:19-20).

- Satan says: *Be popular; push ahead.* God says: "If anyone wishes to come after Me, he must deny himself" (Matthew 16:24 NASB).

- Satan says: *If you don't look after yourself, no one else will. God helps those who help themselves.* God says: "Do nothing from selfishness or empty conceit, but with humility of mind regard one another as more important than yourselves" (Philippians 2:3-4 NASB).

- Satan says: *I can't be happy unless I'm married* (or: *I can't be happy unless I'm single*). God says: "I have learned to be content in whatever circumstances I am" (Philippians 4:11 NASB).

- Satan says: *Eat, drink, and be merry, for tomorrow we die.* God says: "Man does not live on bread alone, but on every word that comes from the mouth of God" (Matthew 4:4).

- Satan says: *If it feels good, do it.* God says: "Not my will, but Yours be done" (Luke 22:42 NASB).

- Satan says: *Everything is relative.* God says: "Your word is truth" (John 17:17).

We could go on, but the point is clear. We must have a plumb line of Scripture against which we can examine the philosophies, premises, and suggestions that we run into every day. A carpenter can't build a house without a plumb line. If he tries to eyeball it and build it according to what looks good in his own eyes, he will wind up with a crooked house. He must have a standard that is inviolate. Regardless of what he feels or how it looks as he's going along, if he sticks to that plumb line, he will wind up with a straight house.

So it is with life. We must look at the Word of God as the plumb line by which everything is measured. A lie is nothing but a lie against the truth. Without the plumb line of Scripture, we have no way of knowing what is truth and what is error.

Once error is identified, the only way to dispel it is with truth—just like the only way to dispel darkness is with light. After all, we don't pay darkness bills. We don't have the Dallas Power and Dark Company. It takes light to dispel the condition of darkness. It's the same spiritually: It takes truth to dispel the condition of error.

Spiritual Truth Is Spiritually Taught

There's a big difference between knowing what something *says* and knowing what it *means*. Millions of Christians know what the Bible says. But many do not know what it means because that can only be revealed by the Spirit. Man's pride rebels against the idea that he cannot understand spiritual truth on his own, but this is what the Bible clearly says:

> The man without the Spirit does not accept the things that come from the Spirit of God, for they are foolishness to him, and he cannot understand them, because they are spiritually discerned (1 Corinthians 2:14).

The reason why is very simple. There is no human alive who can read another man's mind, and if we cannot know what another human being is thinking, how much less can we ever know what God is thinking? First Corinthians 2:11 reminds us of this:

> For who among men knows the thoughts of a man except the man's spirit within him? In the same way no one knows the thoughts of God except the Spirit of God.

How then can God teach us His thoughts? "We have not received the spirit of the world but the Spirit who is from God, that we may understand *what God has freely given us*" (verse 12). Man does not need the enlightening ministry of the Holy Spirit to understand the law; the law was given specifically for the natural man. We need the Holy Spirit to open our minds to the things having to do with the unfathomable riches of His love and grace, those things that "God has *freely* given us." Those truths are described in 1 Corinthians 2:9 this way: "No eye has seen, no ear has heard, no mind has conceived what God has prepared for those who love Him."

In order to understand the things that God wants to teach us regarding His grace, we must have a humble, teachable attitude, for "God opposes the proud but gives grace to the humble" (James 4:6). Just as the same sun that melts wax hardens clay, the same message of God's grace that softens the heart of the humble hardens the proud. The proud cannot receive grace because the proud *will not* receive grace. This offer of grace is offensive to the proud heart. That is why an uneducated but humble person will receive far more genuine and intimate knowledge of God Himself than a highly educated but arrogant theologian.

When we humbly and dependently allow the Spirit to teach us, we will know the truth. When we are so busy doing spiritual activities that we cannot hear what the Spirit is saying, then we become candidates for falling into error. That was my problem. I was so busy with spiritual activities—good things—that I didn't realize that error had crept into my thinking. I needed to be still and listen to the Spirit. I needed to go back to the Word with an open heart and hear what God was saying.

That's when I discovered the incredible liberty that we have as Christians. We have been set free to enjoy life in all its fullness! That freedom provides us with the means to become who we really want to be: holy people with hearts for God. In our own power, we can never make it. All of our human efforts ultimately end in frustration.

But there is a way that leads to life. This way is founded on the work of Jesus Christ, beginning with the crucifixion and continuing through to His resurrection. Let's look at the work of Christ with fresh eyes and see the incredible implications it has for our lives today. I pray that in our journey you, too, will experience freedom in Christ and begin to enjoy the full inheritance that is yours as a child of God.

3

MAN ALIVE!
THE NEGLECTED HALF
OF THE GOSPEL

L ate one night as I was drifting off to sleep, I was jolted by the harsh ring of the telephone. It was a neighbor, apologizing for the late hour, but asking for help. "What's the matter, Sue?" I asked.

"It's Stan," she answered in a low and tired voice. "He's drunk again. Please come over and talk to him."

Wearily, I climbed out of bed and dressed. Stan again! I wondered what I could say to him tonight when, quite frankly, I had already told him everything I knew.

In my first two years as a Christian, I became quickly involved in all kinds of ministries, from evangelism to teaching to counseling. I saw God do wonderful things in people's lives, but Stan was a mystery to me. Sixty-five years old, Stan had been an alcoholic since his college days. He was always open to hearing about Jesus Christ and about His offer of forgiveness of sins and a new way of life. Stan had even walked the aisle of a local church to profess his personal faith in Christ. But nothing seemed to happen to him. It was as if something was keeping the message from getting through. The drinking continued just as before, with all its degrading results.

In those days I had the tremendous experience of sharing the gospel with hundreds of people, and it seemed that most of them experienced an immediate turnaround. But in the case of someone like Stan, someone who accepted the message without being changed afterward, I didn't really know what to do next except to share the same message again and hope that it would "take" this time.

Stan's wife, Sue, on the other hand, was becoming visibly free and healed of her own drinking dependency following her acceptance of Christ. It was a joy to see her growing strong in faith, experiencing inner peace as never before. How was it that two people, both apparently sincere, displayed such contrasting effects of believing the same message? Why did it seem to work for her and not for him?

These questions puzzled me as I walked down the dark street to their home. I never doubted the power of God or the truth of the gospel. I had seen too much of that power in my own life and in the lives of the people I had led to Christ. To me it was like walking into a room, flipping on the light switch, and nothing happening. It would never occur to me to say, "Electricity is a failure." Decades of use have proven the reliability and power of electricity. Therefore, if the lights don't go on, there must be some bad connection on my end of it.

"Lord," I prayed, "there's nothing wrong with You. There's got to be something wrong with Stan, but I have no idea what the problem is, or even where to start. If I am going to help him tonight, You've got to put some words in my mouth…give me some direction…something."

God was going to answer my prayer that night, and more. Years later He would recall this experience to my mind to help me put the pieces of my own life together. Today I hear people almost every night on our nation-wide call-in radio program *People to People* describe virtually the same experience, and I am thankful that I now know the answer that will set them free!

On that night, though, I knocked on the door without a clue as to what I was going to say. Sue answered, greeted me with a quiet "Thank you," and gestured to the living room. There was Stan, a heartbreaking sight in his drunken condition, with the familiar empty expression, lurching movements, and slurred speech. With an attitude of total dependency upon the Lord to guide me, I sat down to talk to him.

For a long time we covered the same territory that we had discussed many times before, making no apparent progress. Suddenly, without any premeditation whatsoever, I asked Stan a question that I had never asked before. It went like this: "Stan, when you accepted Christ, which Jesus did you believe in?"

He looked at me with a puzzled expression. "What do you mean?"

> "Are you willing to...accept the living Christ, the One who has the power to change your life from within?"

"Did you have in your mind an honorable man named Jesus of Nazareth who lived 2000 years ago in a place called Palestine? The historical man who performed miracles, made the blind to see, and the deaf to hear? The man who taught people to love one another, and eventually died on a cross? In other words, Stan, did you accept Jesus the *man*? Or did you accept Jesus Christ the *God* who became a man, who was raised again from the dead? He who is Lord and is alive today? The Lord Jesus Christ who offers to come and live inside of you and give His very life to you?"

Stan's eyes seemed to clear a little as he looked up at me intently. He said, "I received the Jesus who was a man 2000 years ago."

"Then the question is, Stan—are you willing tonight to put your full trust in Jesus *the God*? Not just accept the fact that there once was a good man who walked on the face of the earth, who you're trying to imitate, but to accept the fact that this is the Lord God Himself who is alive today and wants to live in you? Are you willing to get on your knees with me right now, Stan, and accept the living Christ, the One who has the power to change your life from within?"

Stan immediately responded yes. We knelt together, and in his half-drunken state, he trusted in the living Christ. I looked into his face and saw a new man! After being an alcoholic for more than 40 years, Stan was totally freed of his dependency that night.

This isn't to say that all Stan's problems went away instantly. His drinking had cost him his job, and he experienced a terribly frustrating series of rejections initially. But in the midst of trials and tribulations that would be enough to discourage almost anyone, Stan kept trusting God with his life. I thought of him often, and once on a trip back to California I called and invited him to get together with me.

I marveled at God's healing power as I looked at this 70-year-old man standing before me, straight and tall, and compared him with the memory of the broken, defeated man I knew just five years before. Stan's story was an unforgettable example of the grace and power of Jesus Christ, who not only restored Stan spiritually, but enabled him to become the owner of a thriving business. This was a true miracle: the transformation of an insecure, fearful, angry man running from reality into this firm, clear-eyed, peaceful, happy man. Once a burden to his loved ones, Stan was now a consistent, loving husband who was dedicated to the service of other people because of his love for God.

Hearing the Word of Life

But there was another aspect of this story that I couldn't quite grasp, some elusive key to a lock I couldn't identify. On that night five years before, as I had probed into Stan's understanding of the gospel, I learned a vivid lesson on communication: Communication is not just what you mean to *say*; it is what a person *hears*. Though he had learned to speak much of the Christian "language," Stan had not actually "heard" the true gospel. The message he was hearing was this: Being a Christian meant accepting the moral teachings of a great man who lived 2000 years ago and promising to imitate him. When I spotted the error and corrected the message, he was transformed. But it's not always easy to identify the missing link. It often takes a lot of probing to find the error that is the stumbling block to understanding.

A few years later, as I wondered what would cause a busy, outwardly successful Christian worker to be driving down the freeway to work with tears streaming down his cheeks, I remembered Stan. "Where am I missing the message?" I wondered. "Where am I failing to hear what God is saying?" And then God opened my eyes to see the answer. In the midst of that hard time of my life, running furiously on the treadmill of unsatisfying Christian service, a single verse of Scripture began to bang incessantly at my mind. It was Romans 5:10: "For if, when we were God's enemies, we were reconciled to Him though the death of His Son, how much more, having been reconciled, shall we be saved through His life!"

From the time I received Christ, Romans had been one of my favorite books of the Bible. I had read it dozens of times. But this verse suddenly jumped out at me as if I had never seen it before. What did "life" have to do with anything?

If you had asked me any time in those first ten years as a Christian how I was saved, I would have answered, "Through Jesus Christ's death on the cross." I have since noticed the same thing in the vast majority of other Christians I have met. Ask people, "What does it mean to be saved?" and in most cases you will hear an answer like this: "Jesus died for my sins, so there will be a place for me in heaven." Ask, "What is the significance of Christ's death on the cross?" People will quickly answer, "He died for the forgiveness of my sins." Ask, "What is the significance of Christ's *resurrection?*" and in my experience you will usually get dead silence.

Occasionally, someone will say that His resurrection proved Him to be the Son of God, and this is partially correct. But ask, "How does His resurrection apply to our everyday lives?" and you will find that few people seem to know. We Christians are sometimes absolute geniuses at overlooking the obvious. What is the most obvious implication of the word *resurrection?* The restoration of LIFE!

Perhaps you have had the experience of having a word called to your attention for the first time. Suddenly you begin finding that word again while you're online, in conversations, on billboards—seemingly behind every bush! You know, of course, that the word was there all the time; you were just unconscious of it. That's what my experience was with the word *life* in the Bible. Suddenly it was everywhere! It seemed as if God had snuck in and rewritten the Bible when I wasn't looking. The Gospel of John, especially, seemed to be filled with the word *life*.

There was John 10:10: "I came that they may have LIFE, and have it abundantly" (NASB). John 5:24 said, "Whoever hears My word and believes Him who sent Me has eternal LIFE and will not be condemned; he has crossed over from death to LIFE." Even familiar John 3:16 looked brand-new: "For God so loved the world that He gave His one and only Son, that whoever believes in Him shall not perish but have eternal LIFE."

Why Do People Need "Life"?

Seeing this raised many other questions in my mind. Jesus Christ said He came to give life. What kind of person needs life? The answer was obvious: only the dead. Again, verses leaped to my attention. For example, Ephesians 2:1: "As for you, you were *dead* in your transgressions and sins." Before, if asked what the problem of mankind was, I would always have discussed man's sinfulness and need for God's forgiveness. Now this is certainly true, but I began to see, through the Scriptures, that man's problem is much deeper. From God's point of view, the problem of man is not just that he is a sinner in need of forgiveness; his greater problem is that he is *dead* and in need of *life.*

As I thought back to Stan, if there was anything that described the transformation I saw in him, this was it. He didn't need more sincerity; he had always been sincere. He didn't need more willpower; he had tried to change with as much determination as I have seen in any man. He didn't need to feel more convicted about his sins; Stan hated himself for what he had become through alcohol. What Stan had been lacking, what God had given him the night Sue called me to come over, was LIFE. It's no wonder that nothing had worked before. He had been dead. But once Stan had been raised to life, everything changed. What I had seen in Stan was the difference between a dead man and a living one.

God's Purpose for Man's Creation

I was forced to rethink my understanding of the entire Bible, all the way back to Genesis and the creation of man. We are told in Genesis 1:27 that "God created man in His own image, in the image of God He created him; male and female He created them." This was a very familiar verse to me, as it is to most people, but I never stopped to think about what it means. The Bible teaches that God is a spirit, without a body or physical form. Therefore, this verse can't be saying that we look like God.

There are other forms of life that God created. The animal kingdom, for example, possesses what the Bible calls a soul—conscious life expressed through mind, emotions, and will. What makes a man different from an animal? What could it mean that man was created in God's image? I found the answer in the spiritual aspect of man. The human spirit is the part of man that enables him to relate to and know God, and is the source of his inner drives for love, acceptance, meaning, and purpose in life. Man's spirit was created to be united with God's

Spirit and was the means through which he originally enjoyed perfect fellowship with God.

The existence of the human spirit explains the differences between man and the animal kingdom. Take a dog as an example. What does it take to make a dog happy? You give him a place to sleep, food, water, maybe scratch his back a little, and he is satisfied. Do you ever see him sitting with a thoughtful look on his face asking, "Why am I here? What does all this mean?" Do you see him in depression, pushing his bone aside and complaining, "There must be more to life than this"? Of course not. But there is nothing more human than the asking of these questions. Because we have physical bodies with physical needs, there are similarities, but sometime in the life of every human being he begins asking, "Who am I? Why am I here? What is the meaning of life?" That is the working of the human spirit.

God wanted His relationship with man to be a *love* relationship, received and expressed back to Him through the agency of *faith*. Therefore, unlike the animal kingdom, which is governed by an internal behavior mechanism that we call "instinct," man had to be given a free will, because love can only be possible where man is free to choose.

Through this free relationship—God and man united in spiritual life—God had access into Adam's soul (teaching his mind, controlling his emotions, and directing his will) and thereby totally influenced his behavior. As a result of this relationship, every thought, emotion, word, and deed of Adam and Eve were a perfect representation of the God who created them! They were then truly fulfilling their God-ordained purpose in life: walking in a dependent love relationship with their Creator and, through that relationship, *bearing a full, visible representation of the invisible God.*

Here, finally, was the answer to being created "in God's image." Not a physical image, nor mere intelligence, but the display of a certain kind of life—*God's life!* And naturally, since neither Adam nor Eve were God, that life *in* them was totally determined by their free decision to remain in that dependent relationship.

Imagine some intelligent space creature from another planet coming to visit earth and desiring to find out what God is like. How can you see an invisible God? The best advice he could receive would be, "Man is created in God's image. Go observe Adam and Eve, and you'll see what

God is like." If he would do so, our imaginary space creature would go home with the knowledge of the nature and character of God—through observing man, who is created in His image!

Choosing the Lie over Life

Because Adam and Eve's relationship with God was based on love, there had to be a point of decision where they demonstrated that their love of God was freely given. That was the meaning of God's single prohibition: "But from the tree of the knowledge of good and evil you shall not eat, for in the day that you eat from it you will surely die" (Genesis 2:17 NASB). Satan, in the form of a serpent, tempted Eve, saying,

> You surely will not die! For God knows that in the day that you eat from it your eyes will be opened, and you will be like God, knowing good and evil (Genesis 3:4-5 NASB).

This story has been cartooned and ridiculed so much over the years that it is no wonder I missed its real significance, but it contains the explanation of man's deepest needs today. The real meaning of the temptation presented to Adam and Eve lies in the serpent's phrase, "in the day that you eat from it...*you will be like God.*" They were offered the chance (the lie) to step outside of their dependent faith relationship with God, and to assume an independent status—actually, to become their own gods, totally self-sufficient.

In effect, what Satan was saying was, "You don't need God to be a man! Be your own gods! You don't need anyone else to tell you what is right and wrong. You can decide for yourself what is good and evil, and you can begin right here by asserting your independence."

God had said, "In the day that you eat from it, you will surely *die.*" The Bible records that Adam actually lives 930 years. Adam and Eve didn't die physically that day, but by believing Satan's lie and calling God a liar, *they did die spiritually*! God, honoring their free choice, withdrew His life from them, and left them spiritually dead.

A Matter of Life and Death

You will often hear people say, "All men are created in God's image," but let's think that through. *Adam* was created in God's image, but in Genesis 5:1,3 we read:

In the day when God created man, He made him in the likeness
of God…When Adam had lived one hundred and thirty years,
he became the father of a son *in his own likeness, according to his
image,* and named him Seth (NASB).

Two spiritually dead parents could not pass on what they no longer
possessed themselves: spiritual life. The law of reproduction is "like begets
like," and ever since, all men and women have been born according to
the tragic results of Adam's choice: dead spiritually.

To see how far man has fallen, imagine what that space creature would
discover if he came to visit earth today! Everything he observed of human
behavior would be to him an expression of what God is. What would he
discover about God if he followed *you* around for a day?

> Finally the puzzle fit together: Jesus Christ, spiritually alive, laid
> down His life *for* us. Why? So that He could give His life *to* us!

As I was thinking through these things, biblical passages that were
previously familiar, but unexciting, began to hit me like hammer blows.
Vague clouds of confusion began to clear. For example, seeing Adam's
spiritual death made me understand for the first time why the virgin
birth of Jesus Christ is significant. It was the only way He could be born
into this world spiritually alive. If He had been born naturally of two
fallen parents, He would have inherited their state of spiritual death and
their sinful human nature. He had to be born alive spiritually because
only then would He have a life to lay down on our behalf.

The issue in salvation is life and death. Finally the puzzle fit together.
Jesus Christ, spiritually alive, laid down His life *for* us. Why? So that He
could give His life *to* us! Why did we need life? Because we were *spiritually
dead*: "You were dead in your transgressions and sins" (Ephesians 2:1).

The Half-Gospel

I realized that for years I had been functioning with basically one-
half of the gospel. I knew how much I needed the forgiveness of sins that
Christ provided for me, and I was profoundly grateful. But while the
message of God's forgiveness through the cross relieves our guilt and gives
us assurance of where we will go when we die, it does not give us power

to live here and now. It is though the *resurrection* of Christ that any man, woman, boy, or girl on the face of the earth who comes to Him in faith *receives His very life* through the indwelling Holy Spirit! *That's* how we live! Therefore, Ephesians 2:4-5 puts it this way:

> But God, being rich in mercy, because of His great love with which He loved us, even when we were *dead* in our transgressions, *made us alive together with Christ* (by grace you have been saved) (NASB).

Running on Empty

Through these truths, I discovered why Christian service had been killing me. I already knew about the Holy Spirit; in fact, I had taught lectures about His ministry in our lives. But I always associated Him with *power*: giving me power to share Christ, power to understand the Bible, power to teach, power to serve. Of course, there is truth in that. But I was missing the single most important aspect of having the Holy Spirit—the fact that through Him I have received *the very life of God.*

As long as I associated the Spirit's ministry only with power, the emphasis was still on *me.* My prayers were most often, "God, help me to do this activity." God may have been providing some help, but I was still doing it. When I was doing it, there was no lasting joy or fulfillment, and eventually I reached a state of total burnout. Finally I learned that Christ did not come to "help" me serve God; *He came to live His life through me!* I am convinced that many Christians are frustrated with their own spiritual lives because of this same error. This is why Paul wrote:

> I have been crucified with Christ and I no longer live, but *Christ lives in me.* The life I live in the body, I live by *faith* in the Son of God, who loved me and gave Himself for me (Galatians 2:20).

Failing to hold on to these truths, the Christian world has become so frantic in its activity that it reminds me of the well-known definition of a fanatic: "A person who redoubles his efforts after he has lost sight of his goals." Over and over we have witnessed the spectacle of people coming forward in a service to recommit their lives. They rededicate, rededicate, and rededicate their lives, and nothing ever changes. In essence, they are coming down to say, "God, I'm really serious this time. This time I'll do it if it kills me!"

To them I say, "Don't worry. It will!" I know, because it killed me. We have simply not come to grips with the fact that it isn't *hard* to live the Christian life. It's *impossible*! Only Christ can live it. And that's why our only hope is to learn that Jesus Christ did not come just to get men out of hell and into heaven; He came to get Himself out of heaven and into men!

No Power to Change

Evangelistic appeals tell people to come forward and receive forgiveness of sins—and then stop there. Too often that is the whole message shared: "Jesus died for your sins. Come receive forgiveness." Therefore, the gospel that people are *hearing* is, "You trust in Jesus so you can go to heaven when you die. Now in the meantime, *shape yourself up!*" And they try, and they fail.

Don't get me wrong. I'm not saying that a person has to understand these things in detail to be saved. We are saved by putting our full trust in Jesus Christ. But because of our failure to share the gospel fully and accurately, we continue to produce people who are Christians but who don't have a clue about how to live the Christian life. And many other people will struggle (sometimes for years!) with assurance of salvation, experiencing terrible guilt and fear.

I talk to many of them five or ten years after their conversion in my counseling office or on the radio. They are going through divorces, their families are a wreck, and they're sick and tired of life—and often mad at God. They say, "Mr. George, I'm saved. I walked an aisle to receive Christ, but my life has not changed one bit. I don't have any reality to my Christian life."

Many of those are the people who, if they don't find an answer, become responsive to extreme fringe groups that emphasize spectacular "spiritual" experiences. It is easy to criticize the unbiblical nature of those teachings while missing the real tragedy of such people. Their need is genuine and their desire is sincere. The Christian life *should* be miraculous. But not knowing about the life that Christ has given them and how to experience it, they feel caught between extremes: either cold, dead, orthodox religion or spine-tingling experience. Given such a choice, a person who is truly hungry will take experience over orthodoxy. Other people end up simply walking away from the faith, possibly even joining a group like "Fundamentalists Anonymous."

The first thing I have learned to do in such cases is to quiz them on their understanding of the gospel. Invariably, I find that they have heard all about Christ's death *for* them, but they are totally in the dark about Christ's life *in* them. Therefore, they have been trying to grind out the Christian life on their own, resulting in failure.

The One Who Is Life

Then there is the story of Robert. He did not know Christ, despite having been exposed to much Christian teaching. He came to church again and again. He listened and listened and listened. But it never seemed to click for him. In fact, his experience was much like Stan's. In the course of recounting his failures, he said, "I've asked God for help many times."

I responded, "Robert, a dead man doesn't need help. A dead man needs life!" He looked at me with wide, surprised eyes, and listened as I explained what God had taught me about the total message of salvation. That salvation is not just something that Christ did *for* us, but it is Jesus Christ Himself living *in* us. It is the process of passing from death to life.

Now *that* was good news! Robert soon received Christ, and his life has never been the same. Like Stan, when he transformed a vague image of a historical person who lived 2000 years ago into the *living Lord Jesus Christ* who is in the business of giving life *today*, he found everything! But "allowing Christ to live through you" sounds like a vague concept to many people. How do you do it? That's what the rest of this book is all about.

4

FORGIVEN TO BE FILLED

Several years ago in Canada I had just completed a seminar lecture on God's forgiveness when a man approached me and introduced himself. He looked about 60 years old, but it was hard to be sure because of his haggard appearance. His eyes were dull and lifeless, his face was covered with deep creases leading down to his slack mouth, and his shoulders were stooped. When he spoke, his voice came forth in a low drone.

"Mr. George," he said, "I really want to believe that God forgives me, but I don't seem to be able to accept it. How can you know that God forgives your sins?"

"Edward, I just spoke for over an hour on God's total forgiveness in Christ. Were you here for the lecture?"

"Yes, I heard what you said, but I just can't believe that God really forgives me." Wondering if Edward was really a Christian, I took some time to find out. He told of how he had accepted Christ as his Savior and Lord at a very early age. Edward's understanding and answers were all solid regarding his personal faith in Christ: He knew beyond a shadow of a doubt that Christ lived in him, and that he was going to spend eternity in heaven after his death. The source of his doubts had to lie elsewhere.

"How long have you been struggling with these doubts about God's forgiveness?" I asked him.

"Ever since I was a child," Edward said sadly. "When I was young, I did something *very wrong*. Every day since then I have begged God to forgive me, but I just can't believe that He has."

I could hardly believe my ears. "Edward, how old are you?"
"Sixty-two."

"Do you mean to tell me that you have been begging God to forgive you for over 50 years?"

He looked me in the eyes with that helpless expression and nodded. "I should have been serving Him for those 50 years, but I have wasted my life. That's why I'm asking you if you think God could ever forgive me."

We Already Have *Everything*

At the time, I thought that Edward's was a unique story. I have since come to know that many, many Christians share the same bondage. They have committed some sin that seems to always be a part of their present, even as the years roll by. It is constantly on their minds, like an ever-present black cloud hanging over them. After a while, guilt becomes an accepted part of their lives; to lose it would be almost like parting with a precious family heirloom.

A Christian like this will never mature. He will never, as long as he is held in the bondage of guilt over a past sin, experience all that Christ has intended for us to experience through His indwelling life. Let me express this in a straightforward manner: *Until you rest in the finality of the cross, you will never experience the reality of the resurrection.*

Second Peter 1:3-9 is a passage that perfectly illustrates this principle. It begins with this incredible news:

> His divine power has given us *everything we need for life and godliness* through our knowledge of Him who called us by His own glory and goodness. Through these He has given us His very great and precious promises, so that through them *you may participate in the divine nature* and escape the corruption in the world caused by evil desires (verses 3-4).

So many Christians start out with Jesus Christ and then go looking for something better, some kind of "advanced Christianity." We will stray into all kinds of tangents looking for the "something more" that will transform our dull existence into spiritual reality. Sometimes it's a desire for something "deeper." But 2 Peter 1:3 says that we have received how many things? It says "*everything* we need for life and godliness."

Christian maturity is not starting out with Jesus, then graduating to something better. The Christian life is starting with Christ, then spending the rest of eternity discovering more and more of what we *already have* in Him, more and more of the wonders of this Person "in whom are hidden all the treasures of wisdom and knowledge" (Colossians 2:3).

This new life, according to 2 Peter 1:4, is translated into our experience through our having become "partakers of the divine nature" (NASB). In other words, it is through the resurrected life of Christ which has been given to you and me: "Christ in you, the hope of glory" (Colossians 1:27).

Trusting that It's *Done*

I was teaching this recently on a call-in radio program and was asked this question by a listener: "If it is true, as you say, that every Christian has received everything he needs, then why don't many Christians experience it? Even Christians who know about Christ living in them?" (To be specific, someone like Edward.) Let's continue in the passage in 2 Peter 1. After teaching that we have everything we need in Christ, Peter exhorts his readers to press on to maturity in verses 5-8:

> For this very reason, make every effort to add to your faith, goodness; and to goodness, knowledge; and to knowledge, self-control; and to self-control, perseverance; and to perseverance, godliness; and to godliness, brotherly kindness; and to brotherly kindness, love. For if you possess these qualities in increasing measure, they will keep you from being ineffective and unproductive in your knowledge of our Lord Jesus Christ.

No one attains these qualities at a single stroke. They are marks of maturity that we will be growing in as we learn to live by faith in the indwelling Lord Jesus Christ. But what about an Edward? "Ineffective" and "unproductive" are two words that describe his life pretty accurately. What is it that can block this process of maturity from happening? The answer is given in verse 9: "But anyone who does not have them, he is nearsighted and blind, *and has forgotten that he has been cleansed from his past sins.*"

There's the answer! It's another variation on the theme—if truth sets you free, then it is error that binds you. In this case, a failure to recognize and trust that the sin issue between you and God is over will effectively stop your spiritual growth in Christ. It's really not complicated. The process of spiritual maturity is simply our learning to turn more and more areas of our lives over to Christ through faith. The past is over; the future isn't here yet. Therefore, living by faith can only be done in the *present*.

> We must come to the biblical conviction that the forgiveness of our sins is not just some "heavenly bookkeeping" that will enable us to slip into heaven some day.

If Satan, on the other hand, can keep us preoccupied with the *past* through dredging up our feelings of guilt over past sins, then we can never be free to trust Christ as we walk through life today. Besides, how can we trust Christ with our lives if we are unsure of His attitude toward us? Most of us have been taught from an early age that God is holy and "hates sin." If I have committed sins, how can I approach Him with confidence?

The only solution is an understanding of, and a total trust in, the fact that Jesus Christ did it all at the cross; that the sin issue between man and God is truly over. We must come to the biblical conviction that the forgiveness of our sins is not just some "heavenly bookkeeping" that will enable us to slip into heaven some day; God's forgiveness is a *present reality* that enables us to concentrate on walking daily with a loving and accepting God who desires to live through us. Ephesians 1:7 says, "*In Him we have* redemption through His blood, *the forgiveness of sins*, in accordance with the riches of God's grace." Forgiveness is not something we might have, or have on some days and not on others; forgiveness is something the Christian lives in continually, just like we live in and breathe the air. "In Him, we *have*...the forgiveness of sins." It is written in the *present tense*.

The Past Is Past

What a tragedy to look at a man like Edward, who believed that he had wasted his life because of a single past failure. He was in bondage because of error; the solution was truth.

"Edward," I said, "do you have any children?"

"Yes," he answered, "three."

"Did any of those children ever do anything wrong?"

"Well, yes, many times."

"Did you forgive them?"

"Yes, of course."

"Edward, what if on one of those occasions when your child did something wrong, you forgave him, and he refused to believe you, but came every day bringing up the subject again? 'Daddy, are you *sure* that you forgive me for that?' On and on, every day: 'Are you *sure* you forgive me, Daddy? Are you sure?' Tell me, Edward, as a father how would that make you feel?"

Edward creased his brow in a pained expression. "It would break my heart," he said.

"Then, Edward, don't you think it's about time you stopped breaking the heart of God? Do you remember how John the Baptist identified Jesus? 'Look, the Lamb of God, who *takes away* the sin of the world!' (John 1:29). Don't you see, Edward, that God made His Son become sin for you, so that you could become righteous in Him? Don't you think it's about time you stopped insulting the Spirit of God who has written dozens of promises in the Bible that teach that He has forgiven *all* your sins, once and for all?"

Edward squinted and cocked his head in thought. "I never thought about it that way," he said.

"Edward, look at this," I said. I pointed him to Colossians 2:13-14:

> When you were dead in your sins and in the uncircumcision of your sinful nature, God made you alive with Christ. He forgave us *all* our sins, having cancelled the written code, with its regulations, that was against us and that stood opposed to us; He took it away, nailing it to the cross.

"According to this," I continued, "how forgiven are you in God's sight?"

"Totally," he answered.

"Does God hold any accusations against you?"

"No."

"Do you see why?" I asked. "It's so that you can concentrate on the other half of the gospel, that 'God made you *alive* with Christ.' You've been totally preoccupied with the thing that God is *finished* dealing with—sin—with the result that you've totally neglected what God is trying to do with you *today*—teach you about life!"

"Now I see what I have been doing," Edward said. "I feel so guilty about doubting God."

"Now, let's not start that again!" I said. "Next you're going to beat yourself with guilt because you've been feeling so guilty!" Edward laughed. It was the first time he had so much as cracked a smile.

"Edward, don't you see that every one of us would be doomed except for the unbelievable mercy and grace of God? He had to do it all because we were totally helpless to do anything for ourselves. He knows all about you and your deepest failures. What He wants you to do is to rest in what He has done through the cross—to put it to bed once and for all—so that you can begin to experience what He has done through the resurrection."

Edward looked long and hard at Colossians 2:13-14 in my Bible. Finally he said, "I'd like to pray." Closing his eyes, Edward prayed, "Lord Jesus. All these years I've thought that You hated me because of my failure. I've asked and begged You to forgive me over and over, and I have seen myself as a total failure. But today I'm going to start trusting in Your promise. You have heard me ask You to forgive my sin for the last time. I won't insult You and Your grace again. Now, from this day on, Lord, teach me what it means that You live in me. In the years that I have left, I'm Yours to use however You want."

I'll never forget Edward's prayer, because it was one of the first times that I have seen a man's countenance literally change before my eyes. Edward turned in his legalism lines for a grace face! He looked years younger, even as he looked up at me with his eyes bright and shining with tears. Edward became free from the bondage of guilt through seeing and trusting in the completeness of Christ's work on the cross to deal with our sins. Therefore he finally became free to experience the life of Christ, which had in fact been his since his conversion many years before. His life perfectly illustrates the principle of 2 Peter 1:9: Until you rest in the finality of the cross, you will never experience the reality of the resurrection.

Saved So We Can *Live*

Satan has done a masterful job of keeping the Christian world pre-occupied with the thing that God has dealt with once and for all—sin—and ignorant of the thing that God wants us to be preoccupied with—life! This in no way means that we are to minimize what Jesus did on the cross. Thank God for that! But it is only when we understand that the ultimate goal of salvation was the restoration of life that we can truly appreciate the purpose and meaning of Jesus Christ's death for us on the cross.

The process of canning is an excellent illustration of the two parts of the gospel. Let's say that you are going to preserve some peaches. What is the first thing you have to do? Sterilize the jars. Why the process of sterilization? So that the contents of the jars—the peaches—will be preserved from spoiling.

Imagine a husband coming home and finding his wife boiling jars in the kitchen. "What are you doing, honey?"

"Sterilizing jars."

"Why are you doing that?" the husband asks.

"I just like clean jars," she answers.

The husband is clearly at a loss. "What are you going to do next?" he asks.

"Keep them clean!"

This story doesn't make much sense, does it? You have never seen anyone decorate his kitchen with a sterile jar collection. No, the only reason to sterilize jars is *because you intend to put something in them*. We would never expect to find a person involved in only half the process of canning, just cleansing jars. But we have done this exact thing with the gospel! We have separated God's sterilization process—the cross—from His filling process—Christ coming to live in us through His resurrection!

The Christian world, to a large extent, has been guilty of teaching half a gospel—that is, the cross of Christ which brought us forgiveness of sins. But by separating forgiveness of sins from the message of receiving the life of Christ, we have not only missed out on experiencing life, but we have lost sight of the purpose of forgiveness in the first place. The reason that God had to deal once and for all with the sin issue was so that we could be filled with Christ "without spoiling."

As a matter of fact, there is one final part of the canning process. After sterilizing the jars and filling them with fruit, the jars are *sealed*. Sealing keeps the good things inside and the bad things that would spoil the contents outside. We read in Ephesians 1:13:

> And you also were included in Christ when you heard the word of truth, the gospel of your salvation. Having believed, you were marked in Him with a *seal*, the promised Holy Spirit.

Cleansing, filling, and sealing: a wonderful picture of salvation!

Once for All

Once we see that the goal of salvation is the raising of dead men to life, it is easy to see why Christ had to deal with the sin issue once and for all. This is exactly what the New Testament teaches from beginning to end. For example, notice these verses from three different writers:

> The death He died, He died to sin *once for all*; but the life He lives, He lives to God (Romans 6:10).

> But now He has appeared *once for all* at the end of the ages to do away with sin by the sacrifice of Himself (Hebrews 9:26).

> For Christ died for sins *once for all*, the righteous for the unrighteous, to bring you to God. He was put to death in the body but made alive by the Spirit (1 Peter 3:18).

Sin Is Covered...

The message of God's complete, 100-percent forgiveness in Christ has been a controversial, mind-boggling subject for nearly 2000 years. To prepare the way, God gave Israel the law of Moses with its sacrificial system. Even though these sacrifices were God-ordained, no one was ever made right with God through them. Instead, they were merely a picture of Christ and His finished work on our behalf:

The law is only a shadow of the good things that are coming—
not the realities themselves. For this reason it can never, by the
same sacrifices repeated endlessly year after year, make perfect
those who draw near to worship (Hebrews 10:1).

Forgiveness was different under the law (also called the Old Covenant). It was a good news/bad news situation. Let's say that you are an
Israelite living under the law. All year long God is keeping a record of
your violations of the law, and the entire nation's as well. All year long
you feel the guilt of your sins; you live in fear of God's punishment,
which was threatened for transgressions of the law. But the great Day
of Atonement is coming! The annual day of fasting and praying and
confessing your sins. The day each year when the perfect bull is sacrificed on behalf of the nation. The one and only time that a single mortal
man, representing the whole nation, can enter into the most holy room
of the temple, the Holy of Holies, which represents the very presence
of God. Taking sacrificial blood, the high priest fearfully enters behind
the veil and there sprinkles the blood which covers the nation's—and
your—sins for the previous year.

Two goats are sacrificed as well: One is slain at the altar; the other,
called the scapegoat, becomes the subject of an unusual ceremony. Elders
of the nation place their hands on the head of the goat, symbolizing the
transfer of the nation's sins to the animal. Then, before thousands of witnesses lining the streets, the scapegoat is driven from the city, out into
the wilderness, symbolizing the removal of your sins. You watch with
relief and thanksgiving, the Innocent animal symbolically taking your
guilt away. What relief! That's the good news.

> A man under the law could enjoy the blessing of God's for-
> giveness, but that system provided no final solution.

What's the bad news? Tomorrow your sins begin adding up again.
Next year there will need to be another sacrifice. And the next year. And
the next.

God graciously gave this system to Israel as a means for man to experience relief from the guilt he experienced under the law. The key Old Testament word is *atonement,* which means a covering. Those sacrificial offerings did, indeed, *cover* sins, but they could not *take them away,* "because it is *impossible* for the blood of bulls and goats to *take away* sins" (Hebrews 10:4). A man under the law could enjoy the blessing of God's forgiveness, but that system provided no final solution. It is similar to the use of a credit card, which enables a person to have the benefit today of the coat he wants to buy, without paying cash. That's the good news. But the bad news is that somebody is going to have to pay the tab! The card didn't pay for the coat; it only transferred the debt to an account. That account will still have to be paid.

Sin Is Taken Away!

Then in God's perfect timing, Jesus Christ was introduced to Israel by John the Baptist: "Look, the Lamb of God who *takes away* the sin of the world!" (John 1:29). From that point on, the finished work of Christ is presented in the New Testament in total contrast to the old system:

> And by [God's] will, we have been made holy through the sacrifice of the body of Jesus Christ *once for all.* Day after day every priest stands and performs his religious duties; again and again he offers the same sacrifices, which *can never take away sins.* But when this priest had offered *for all time one sacrifice* for sins, He sat down at the right hand of God (Hebrews 10:10-12).

Relentlessly the New Testament hammers home the message that Jesus Christ offered Himself as one sacrifice for all time. When will we believe it? In contrast to the Old Covenant priests who are pictured as "standing" and making continual sacrifices, Christ is shown as having *sat down.* Why is He seated? Because *"it is finished!"* (John 19:30). The writer of Hebrews reaches the climax of his argument in 10:14: "Because by *one sacrifice* He has made *perfect forever* those who are being made holy." Jesus Christ has done it all!

I find that few Christians can read that verse without flinching and trying to water it down. It is too bold, and the implications are too threatening. Notice that it doesn't say we *act* perfect; this is talking about identity. But the Bible says that *through Jesus Christ* we *have* been made totally acceptable in the eyes of a holy God!

∞

I'll never forget a conversation I had one time with a pastor of a certain denomination that teaches that you can lose your salvation. The more we talked, the more obvious it became to me that this man really did have a good handle on the grace of God, at least intellectually. Finally I looked him right in the eye and said, "Jim, you know the Word of God. You also know how great a work our Lord did at the cross. I think you know too much to really believe that a born-again Christian can lose his salvation."

A sheepish, sly grin grew on Jim's face. Then he said, "You're right, Bob. Jesus Christ has done it all. There's nothing more that needs to be done or can be done to deal with man's sins. I do know that once you've been born again, you can't be unborn." Then he turned serious. "But how could I ever keep my people in line if I taught them that? They would just take that message as a license to sin. So I don't teach it."

I really wonder how many other leaders in church history have done the same thing out of abject fear of "what the people will do." The tragedy is that their fear is unnecessary—*if* they are teaching the entire gospel: not the cross and forgiveness of sins alone, but the cross plus God's gift of the resurrected life of Christ.

God said in the New Covenant, "I will put My laws in their minds and write them on their hearts" (Hebrews 8:10). If salvation was only forgiveness of sins without a change of heart, yes, we would probably take it as a license to sin. But not when Christ lives in us! When we are learning to experience the "abundant life" that Jesus Christ has promised, we become preoccupied with our daily relationship with Him: the One who loved us and gave His life *for* us, so that He could give His life *to* us. But we absolutely have to settle the finality of the cross in our own minds, or we will never be free to discover, experience, and enjoy the reality of the resurrection—real LIFE restored to man!

5

PUTTING THE PIECES TOGETHER

After many years spent talking with people of all denominations from every part of the country, I picture the average Christian's understanding to be much as mine was: like a person with a big box of jigsaw puzzle pieces, each piece representing a Bible verse, a sermon illustration, or a doctrine they have been taught. If you have been a Christian very long at all, you have probably accumulated quite a collection! Especially in twenty-first-century America, which I believe has received more Christian education than any group in the last 2000 years. All those puzzle pieces... *but we don't know how to put them together!*

Have you ever tried to put together a jigsaw puzzle without the cover of the box which shows what the finished picture should look like? You pick up a piece: "Well, it's got a little red, a little green, and a little white in it. But I don't have a clue to what it is." So you pick up another piece that also has some red, green, or white. They don't fit easily, but with a little brute force you can make them stick together. Unfortunately, the union of the two still doesn't look like anything recognizable.

On the other hand, if you have the cover of the box to compare the piece to, you can easily identify where the piece goes. "Now I see," you say. "The red on this piece is part of that barn, the green is part of the tree, and the white is part of the sheet hanging on the line. Oh, here's another part of the barn, and it fits like so." How much easier it is to identify the small pieces when you can put them into a context! And that is exactly what God did for me, through opening my understanding to the "life and death" issue of salvation. He took me back to a bird's-eye view of the whole Bible, which immediately caused hundreds of small pieces that we call verses to fall into place. There weren't any new verses. I knew them all well. But finally I could see where they fit in—without having to apply brute force!

As I have had the pleasure of teaching thousands of people the same life-transforming truths, I have heard them say again and again, "For the first time in my life, I can understand my Bible!" They always say this with a sense of wonder. That shows you that they had, in their hearts, really given up hope of ever understanding the Word of God. A friend of mine said it this way: "It was astonishing to me to discover that Christianity actually makes sense!" That sounds strange, yet I have heard it repeatedly.

⥤

When people are challenged for the first time to examine their understanding of the gospel, there are many predictable questions that they will ask. The following account is a very typical discussion.

I was teaching a seminar when a man named Don said, "Bob, I've been taught that a Christian can lose his salvation. I know that Christ died for our *past* sins, but what about our *future* sins? I don't understand what you mean when you say that Christ *had* to take away *all* sins."

I answered him this way: "Don, let's take your questions in order. First of all, when Christ died for your sins, how many of them were in the future?"

He hesitated a moment. "All of them," he answered.

"They had to be, of course, unless you're more than 2000 years old!" I said, and we laughed. "The problem, Don, is that we are looking at things from the perspective of time, and God is looking at things from the perspective of eternity, which is entirely out of time. We look at the passing of days and years like we watch railroad cars at a crossing—one at a time. But God sees all of time as a person would see the entire train from an airplane overhead—from the engine to the final car."

God's Complete Provision

"At the cross, God took every sin that every man will ever commit and placed them all on Jesus Christ. The Lord Jesus took all the punishment for your and my sins in one action. That's why 1 John 2:2 (alternate rendering) says, 'He is the one who turns aside God's wrath, taking away our sins, and not only ours but also the sins of the whole world.' The theological word is *propitiation*. Have you ever heard of it?"

"I don't even think I could pronounce it!" Don said. "What does that mean?"

"Propitiation means that God the Father was totally *satisfied* with the sacrifice made by His Son. There at the cross, God poured out every ounce of His anger and hatred for sin that you and I deserved so that His justice is totally *satisfied;* except that Jesus took it for us. That's why the Bible says, 'He did it to *demonstrate His justice* at the present time, so as to be *just* and *the one who justifies* the man who has faith in Jesus' (Romans 3:26). That's why there isn't any wrath left for you."

"A man has died of cancer...To save the man, how many problems would you have to solve? Two! You'd have to raise him to life, but you'd also have to cure his cancer."

I could tell the group was thinking hard. "Let's think it through," I continued. "If you were to stand before the judgment seat of God today in your own righteousness, what would be the verdict?"

"Guilty," Don said.

"That's right, and it would be the same for me. Now then, what is the punishment for sin?"

"Death, I guess," Don answered again.

"That's right. Romans 6:23 says, 'For the wages of sin is death.' And Christ took it for you! That's why there isn't any punishment left for you.

"By the way," I continued, "I only quoted the first half of Romans 6:23. Not too many of us seem to know the second half: 'but the gift of God is eternal *life* in Christ Jesus our Lord.' This gets us into the second part of your question about why Christ had to totally deal with the sin issue. Let's imagine that a man has died of a disease—cancer, for example. Don, if you had the power to save the man, how many problems would you have to solve? Two! You'd have to raise him to life, but you'd also have to cure his cancer, wouldn't you?" I paused while they thought it over.

"For example," I went on, "what if you cured his cancer, but did nothing else?"

"He would still be dead," Don answered.

"That's right. You'd just have a healthy dead man on your hands!" Don and I laughed, and I continued. "On the other hand, what if you raised him to life without curing his cancer?"

After a moment's pause, Don answered, "He would just die again."

"You've got it. And that, Don, is a perfect picture of man's condition, from God's point of view, after the Fall. Ever since Adam sinned, the earth has been the land of the walking dead—spiritually dead. What is the disease that killed man? We've already seen it: 'The wages of sin is death.' So from God's point of view, salvation involves the raising of spiritually dead men to life. But before God could give life to the dead, He had to totally eradicate the fatal disease that killed men—sin. So the cross was God's method of dealing with the disease called sin, and the resurrection of Christ was and is God's method of giving life to the dead!"

Don was thoughtful for a minute. "Okay," he said, "I think I'm getting it."

Understanding Security

The rest of the group had been quietly listening to this exchange, but Lynn raised her hand. "I'm still not sure why you can't lose your salvation," she said.

"All right," I answered, "let's first remember what salvation is. From our study, how would you explain it?"

"It's when a person trusts in the Lord Jesus and receives forgiveness of sins and His life," Lynn answered. "The Spirit of God comes to live in you."

"That's good," I said. "Now remember: Adam was created spiritually alive. What caused the Spirit of God to depart from Adam, leaving him spiritually dead?"

"His sin," was her answer.

"Right. Now, Jesus Christ on the cross experienced death, too. Why did He die?"

The group was more hesitant this time. Then Don spoke up, "I guess it was the same thing—sin."

"That's right," I answered. "Second Corinthians 5:21 says, 'God made Him who had no sin *to be sin* for us, so that in Him we might become the righteousness of God.' So we're left with this: Adam died because of his sin. Jesus Christ died because He *became* sin. How can you and I know that we will never die spiritually again, even though we still commit sins as Christians?"

Don was confident now as he answered. "Because the disease has been totally taken away. Our sins have been forgiven."

"Therefore," I concluded, "when the Lord Jesus gives us His resurrected life, it can truly be *eternal* life, because the only thing that could ever cause you to die—sin—has been completely dealt with at the cross. That's how you can know that your salvation is secure forever. Now, knowing that you are secure in Christ, you are free to concentrate on God's greatest priority for you today: learning to experience real life—Christ Himself living through you."

Discussions like these can be a little tough to wade through at times, but there are tremendous benefits. We Christians tend to talk too much in generalities, and this helps to cause the phenomenon where people can speak the Christian "language" but have never really thought through—for themselves, based on the Bible—what they believe. It's when we make ourselves take what the Bible says and carry it all the way to conclusions that we discover the experience that I mentioned earlier in the chapter—where Christianity really makes sense and it works in real life, in the real world.

Enlarging Our View of Salvation

In many cases, Christians' understanding of salvation is not so much *wrong* as *too small*. For example, most people are at least familiar with the word *forgiveness,* but the Bible has much more to say about our salvation than forgiveness.

Reconciliation

One of the major biblical terms that expresses the finality of the sin issue is "reconciliation." It is expressed in 2 Corinthians 5:19: "God was *reconciling the world to Himself* in Christ, not counting men's sins against them. And He has committed to us the message of reconciliation."

The entire world has been reconciled to God through the cross. I read this verse on the radio, and it caused a listener named Bill to ask this question: "Bob, if the whole world is reconciled to God, does that mean that the whole world is saved?"

"That depends, Bill, on your definition of salvation. If salvation is just man's being reconciled to God, the answer would be yes. But that's not salvation, is it?"

After thinking for a moment, Bill said, "No, salvation is when a person receives Jesus Christ Himself; when he is born again."

"Right," I answered. "The word *reconciliation* means that the barrier between God and man—sin—has been taken away. A bridge has been built between man and God. Therefore the only thing that keeps any man from eternal life is his refusal to accept the salvation that God offers. Reconciliation has been accomplished for the whole world through Christ, but that alone is not salvation. That's just half of the coin. The reason that God has removed the sin barrier is so that whosoever will come to Christ by faith can become alive in Him. Colossians 2:13 puts it all together: 'When you were dead in your transgressions and the uncircumcision of your flesh, *He made you alive together with Him, having forgiven us all our transgressions*' (NASB).

"That's why the only sin that will ever send a man to hell is his unbelief. John 3:18 says, 'Whoever believes in Him is not condemned, but whoever does not believe stands condemned already because he has not believed in the name of God's one and only Son.' What does it mean to be condemned already? He remains dead. Because of his sins? No. Because of his unbelief."

This is a shocking message! Many of us are used to thinking of a vengeful, furious God who is just itching to blast men off the face of the earth. But the gospel is actually the announcement of an *accomplished fact*—God's work of reconciliation has *already* taken place! And reconciliation is something that God did *on His own initiative*. He didn't consult anyone—He just did it.

God the Father's Initiative

People talk glibly about "man's search for God." But the gospel is the story of *God's search for man!* This is the fantastic message of Romans 5:6-10. The theme that is hit again and again is God's taking the initiative to bring about reconciliation with men:

> When we were still powerless, Christ died for the ungodly... But God demonstrates His own love for us in this: While we were still sinners, Christ died for us...When we were God's enemies, we were reconciled to Him through the death of His Son (Romans 5:6,8,10).

I have pointed out many times that nobody at the cross asked the Lord Jesus to forgive their sins. But what was His request? "Father, forgive them, for they do not know what they are doing" (Luke 23:34). It was *His action* on *His initiative* that brought about forgiveness for man!

The familiar story of the prodigal son in Luke 15:11-32 gives a perfect picture of God's attitude toward the lost world since the cross. The young man has taken and squandered his inheritance, bringing shame to his father and family. Destitute, he has accepted the lowest possible job for a Jew, feeding filthy swine, in order to stay alive. He has really hit bottom. But what is his father's attitude? He hasn't written the boy off. That father isn't standing with his arms folded, glaring down the road and sputtering, "You just wait until I get my hands on that kid! He's going to pay for what he's done!" No! You can tell the father's attitude by his response when he saw his son returning:

> But while he was still a long way off, his father saw him and was filled with compassion for him; he ran to his son, threw his arms around him and kissed him (Luke 15:20).

The next thing he did was to throw a party.

Now think about it. When that boy was still with the pigs, what stood in the way of his returning to his father? Nothing on the father's part! In fact it's easy to picture that man each day gazing down the road with a longing expression, thinking, "Maybe today my boy will come home." The only thing that kept that boy from his father was the son's own decision: to stay with the pigs or to go home. If there were an evangelist portrayed in the story, his message would have been, "Why are you living with the pigs? Your father loves you. He's not holding any grudges against you. He wants you to come home! Go and be restored to him."

Today, God is calling men to come home, just like the father longed for his prodigal son. In the same chapter, Jesus compares God's attitude toward men to a shepherd who is out diligently searching for a single lost sheep out of a hundred, and to a woman who is carefully sweeping an entire house to find a single precious coin. All three stories conclude with great rejoicing, and Jesus summarizes His point with the statement, "In the same way, I tell you, there is rejoicing in the presence of God over one sinner who repents" (Luke 15:10).

This is the result of Jesus Christ's finished work on the cross. Because He did all that was necessary to remove the offense of sin, when a sinner returns to God he comes home to open arms and rejoicing in heaven. And he comes home to discover real life!

Questions About Our Total Forgiveness

To many people, all this emphasis on total forgiveness and Christ living in you seems threatening because they fear that it will lead people to become complacent about their Christian lives. They hear the phrase "living by faith" and picture lazy people sitting around, waiting for something to happen. The exact opposite is true. As the last chapter showed, it is an emphasis on the cross and forgiveness of sins *to the exclusion of teaching people about sharing Christ's resurrected life* that really leads to complacency.

The Basis for Our Motivation

Let me share an illustration. Let's imagine that a king made a decree in his land that there would be a blanket pardon extended to all prostitutes. Would that be good news to you if you were a prostitute? Of course it would. No longer would you have to live in hiding, fearing the sheriff. No longer would you have a criminal record; all past offenses are wiped off the books. So the pardon would definitely be good news. But would it be any motivation at all for you to change your lifestyle? No, not a bit.

But let's go a little further with our illustration. Let's say that not only is a blanket pardon extended to all who have practiced prostitution, but the king has asked you, in particular, to become his bride. What happens when a prostitute marries a king? She becomes a queen. *Now* would you have a reason for a change of lifestyle? Absolutely. It doesn't take a genius to realize that the lifestyle of a queen is several levels superior to that of a prostitute. No woman in her right mind would go back to her previous life.

As long as a half-gospel continues to be taught, we are going to continue producing Christians who are very thankful that they will not be judged for their sins, but who have no significant self-motivation to change their behavior. That's why so many leaders have to use the hammer of the law and suffocating peer pressure to keep their people in line.

But what is the church called in the New Testament? The bride of Christ! The gospel message is in effect a marriage proposal. And just as the prostitute became a queen by marrying the king, guilty sinners have become sons of God by becoming identified with Christ. It is that relationship and our new identity that becomes our motivation, and it is motivation that comes from *within*.

The Issue of Identity

Being made into a new creation is like a caterpillar becoming a butterfly. Originally an earthbound crawling creature, a caterpillar weaves a cocoon and is totally immersed in it. Then a marvelous process takes place, called metamorphosis. Finally a totally new creature—a butterfly—emerges. Once ground-bound, the butterfly can now soar above the earth. It now can view life from the sky downward. In the same way, as a new creature in Christ you must begin to see yourself as God sees you.

> All the time I hear Christians referring to themselves
> as "just an old sinner saved by grace"…That's like calling
> a butterfly a converted worm.

If you were to see a butterfly, it would never occur to you to say, "Hey, everybody! Come look at this good-looking converted worm!" Why not? After all, it *was* a worm. And it was "converted." No, now it is a new creature, and you don't think of it in terms of what it was. You see it as it is now—a butterfly.

In exactly the same way, God sees you as His new creature in Christ. Although you might not always act like a good butterfly—you might land on things you shouldn't, or forget you are a butterfly and crawl around with your old worm buddies—the truth of the matter is, you are never going to be a worm again!

This is why the usual New Testament word for a person in Christ is *saint*, meaning "holy one." Paul, for example, addressed nearly all his letters to the "saints." Yet all the time I hear Christians referring to themselves as "just an old sinner saved by grace." No! That's like calling a butterfly a converted worm. We were sinners and we were saved by grace, but the Word of God calls us saints from the moment we become identified with Christ.

Some people ask, "But I still commit sins. Doesn't that make me a sinner?"

I answer, "It depends on whether your identity is determined by your behavior—what you do—or by who you are in God's eyes." Do you see how we have continued to do as Christians what the world does by determining a person's identity based on his behavior? The only way to get free of this is to do what Paul wrote in Colossians 3:1-3:

> Since, then, you have been raised with Christ, set your hearts on things above, where Christ is seated at the right hand of God. *Set your minds on things above,* not on earthly things. For you died, and your life is now hidden with Christ in God.

Living Out Who You Are

Throughout the New Testament the dominant motivation for our living godly lives is the love and grace of God. Ephesians, for example, is very representative of Paul's letters and of the New Testament as a whole. The whole letter can be outlined by two key verses. The first verse is: "Praise be to the God and Father of our Lord Jesus Christ, who has blessed us in the heavenly realms with every spiritual blessing in Christ" (Ephesians 1:3). Chapters one through three are really a commentary on this verse, describing the greatness of God's mercy toward us, and who we are as a result. Then Paul turns his attention to motivation and behavior: "As a prisoner for the Lord, then, I urge you to live a life worthy of the calling you have received" (Ephesians 4:1). The rest of the letter, chapters four through six, expounds on practical areas of applying this verse. There is plenty of exhortation to action in Ephesians, but don't miss the fact that Paul has spent three chapters establishing *why* we should live this certain type of life.

To me, one of the greatest and most concise examples of New Testament motivation is found in Ephesians 5:8: "For you were once darkness, but now you are light in the Lord. Live as children of light." A good paraphrase would be, "You once were a worm; now you are a butterfly. Fly like a butterfly!"

If you were to ask the apostle Paul, "Why should I live as a child of light?" his answer would be very simple and practical: "Because that's what you are." Doesn't that make perfect sense? Yes—assuming that you know you are a child of light. But too many Christians are trying to live the Christian life—trying to act like butterflies—while thinking in their hearts that they are still worms.

The Bible says, "If anyone is in Christ, he is a new creation: the old has gone, the new has come!" In the following chapters, we will explore those "new things" that God has graciously given us—beginning with the crucial issue of our new identity in Christ.

6

TOWARD A PROPER
SELF-IMAGE

The small boy, not quite three years old, skipped down the imposing corridors. Armed servicemen, the best of the best, took no notice of the child who ran past their assigned posts. The boy passed several staff members on his way, who likewise took little notice except for an occasional smile. Passing a secretary's desk, the little boy did not acknowledge her wave, intent as he was on his goal. In front of the door stood another armed sentry. But the guard made no movement to hinder the progress of the child who opened the door and went inside. With a grin, the boy ran across the carpet of the Oval Office and climbed into the lap of the most powerful man in the world. Influential cabinet members had to wait to continue their discussion as President John F. Kennedy and his son, John-John, exchanged good-morning hugs and kisses.

The years of the Kennedy administration are memorable to me because they were one of the few times that there have been small children living at the White House. I remember seeing on the news how the president loved his children and delighted to include them in his day, even while attending to matters that concerned the future and safety of the entire world's population. The contrast has always struck me: the most powerful man in the world, and the little boy who could stroll past secretaries, staff members, and security guards and bound into his father's arms.

Can you imagine someone objecting? "Now, wait just a minute! Don't you know who that man is? He is the president of the United States, the leader of the greatest nation on earth. You can't just waltz in here anytime you want. And you certainly can't be sitting in his lap! Who do you think you are?" John-John would have just looked up at his challenger with a surprised look. Then, with a grin of total confidence, he would have said, "He's my daddy!" You see, John-John knew who his father was, and he knew who he was.

It's a Matter of Relationship

The tragedy of modern-day Christians is our utter ignorance of who we are in Christ. After Jesus Christ has done everything necessary to make us acceptable to a holy God, after He has given us His very life to experience every day, too many of us still thrash around in doubt as to whether God will really hear our prayers, whether we're "worthy" to be used by God in the ministry, or simply whether God really and truly loves us. "I mean, how could God love me, knowing what I am really like?" we think in our hearts.

I know from firsthand experience that these doubts haunt the lives of multitudes of Christians. I have heard them time and time again in thousands of hours of personal counseling and teaching Bible studies. I hear people each weeknight on live radio ask the same questions and express the same doubts.

In seminars I have passed out index cards and asked the audience to write their answers to a single question: "How do you feel God sees you right now?" The answers that I have collected are pitiful. Here are some actual samples: "A being that is a sinner, that tries not to sin, but ends up sinning." "God must see me often as hypocritical. I've learned to play the role of 'Christian,' but my heart is not truly, fully, yielded to God in every area of my life." "He sees a very troubled and misinformed baby." "I think He feels sick when He sees me; disgusted, disappointed." "He is sickened at me."

It is not easy for people who think God is seeing them this way to apply verses like Hebrews 4:16, which says, "Let us then approach the throne of grace with *confidence*, so that we may receive mercy and find grace to help in our time of need." At the heart of these persons' need, as well as John-John Kennedy's confidence, is the issue of *identity*. Who are you? And how do you determine who you are?

Imagine yourself for a moment living on a desert island without ever having seen another human being. Suddenly a voice comes out of heaven and asks, "Who are you?" You wouldn't have the slightest idea how to answer. Then, a ship appears on the horizon and soon arrives at the island. A man splashes to shore. He runs to you, embraces you, and shouts, "At last! I have found my long-lost child!"

"Who are you?" you ask.

"I'm John Doe. And you are my child, Pat."

Again, the voice out of heaven asks, "Who are you?"

Now you know the answer. "I'm Pat Doe. John Doe's child."

Looking in the Wrong Places

A person has no identity apart from his relationship with someone or something else. That's why we will latch onto practically anything in our desperate need to discover who we are. People will determine their identities through their appearance, occupation, abilities, family relationships, friends, denominational affiliation, and many other ways. The common denominator of all these human attempts to discover identity is that they are all temporal—they can change with the winds.

A child colors a small picture with crayons and takes it to her mother. Mom oohs and aahs and says, "Susie, that's wonderful! You're a genius! I'll bet you're going to be an artist one day."

Susie goes away thinking, "If Mom liked that little picture so well, think how much she would like it if I drew a big one on the wall!" So off she goes, finds the biggest wall in her room, and proceeds with her masterpiece.

A little while later, there is a shriek. "Susie! You stupid kid! What were you thinking about...?" This is very confusing to a child. One minute, you're a genius. The next minute, you're stupid.

By the time we have grown up, we have likely gained a lot of experience confirming that the opinions of other people are a shaky way to determine who we are. Professional athletes strike me as the ultimate example. Make a great play, and people will throw a parade for you. Blow the play, and they will likely hound you about it for the rest of your life. The same thing holds true in marriage, as well. If someone were to ask, "What does your wife think of you?" my answer would probably be, "What hour?" It can change at any given moment.

Many people determine their identity by their profession: "I am a businessman." But what happens if you get fired or retire? Who are you then? "I am a mother," say many women. But what happens when the kids grow up and leave home to lead their own adult lives? Who are you then? "I am an athlete...musician...model." Determining your identity by the looks or the functioning of your body is surely building your life on sand. There are injuries and illnesses that can attack you. There's continual, intense competition—maybe someone just a little better than you is just around the corner. At the very least, there is the inevitable aging process.

There is only one way to determine your identity that cannot be shaken, one foundation that cannot be taken away from you: "I am a child of God." Now you might be a child of God who happens to be a businessman...or a mother...or an athlete. But the core source of your identity is your relationship with your God and Father. Only in this way can you ever begin to discover true security.

Trapped by Labels

All of us carry the scars of past experiences. Just think of kids on a school playground, about how unkind they are to each other. Listen to the nicknames: Porky, Dumbo, Stupid, Stinky, Retardo. Think of the labeling: "He's a slow learner." "She's developmentally challenged." Remember the vindictive epithets: wop, kike, greaser, wetback, nigger. Yes, this world is not a kind place to live! And many of us are still hurting and wrestling with those memories as we are becoming grandparents.

After one seminar I was approached by an elderly gentleman who was just beaming with excitement. "I want to thank you so much," he said, "because at this seminar I have learned for the first time who I am in Christ." I asked him about his story and he said, "I am 87 years old. When I was a little boy, the other children called me 'monkey-face' and made fun of me. All my life I've struggled with my self-image. Now I can say that Jesus Christ has set me free!"

You are probably wondering what he looked like. He was quite handsome! But as we saw in chapter 2, our emotions will respond to what is in our minds, without being able to discern between truth and error. Can you imagine? For *over 80 years* this man had been trying to escape being "monkey-face." What a shame, and yet many people share the same experience.

Focused on Failure

As if the usual struggles for identity that we all experience were not enough, millions of people become labeled with an identity that focuses on their greatest weakness. One day a young man came into my office for a counseling appointment. He flinched and shook. He was obviously on some kind of drug. He introduced himself this way: "My name is Jimmy. I am a paranoid, manic-depressive schizophrenic." I looked at him and said, "That's really a marvelous self-image! I imagine that you can hardly wait to get up in the morning so you can look in the mirror and say, 'Hi there, Jimmy, you old paranoid, manic-depressive schizophrenic!' Who hung that label on you?" After his initial surprise, Jimmy explained his history. He had been under the treatment of psychiatrists and psychologists since he was 18 years old. His father had originally taken him because he had been "depressed." But with each new counselor, their diagnosis had grown more complicated. Jimmy blundered through the years, failing at work, marriage, and life. His dependency upon the drugs grew as he resigned himself to his circumstances.

> Jimmy and I worked hard to plow through the errors in his life one by one, but it was settling the issue of identity that enabled change to happen.

"Jimmy," I began, "I agree that you have made some poor decisions in life, and we'll work on those. But I am most concerned right now with who you think you are. Are you a Christian?" Yes, he answered. "Are you in Christ?" Yes. "Does Christ live in you?" Yes. "Then let's determine who you are based on who *God* says you are! Do you think that if God were introducing you around the kingdom of heaven He would say, 'This is Jimmy: the paranoid, manic-depressive schizophrenic'? No! God would say, 'This is My beloved son, Jimmy'! When God looks at you, He sees a child of His who is totally forgiven, perfect in His sight because you are in Christ and indwelt by the Holy Spirit of God, and He sees you as a person who has also made some pretty poor decisions, and who has believed a lot of lies based on the thinking of this world."

Jimmy was really perking up by this point. "You know, Bob," he said. "God has been showing me the same thing lately as I have been reading the Bible, but I didn't know how to put it into words." Jimmy and I worked hard to plow through the errors in his life one by one, but it was settling the issue of identity that enabled change to happen. We studied the Bible extensively until Jimmy saw for himself who he was in God's eyes. He found a doctor who helped wean his body off the drugs, and he improved visibly day by day. Today Jimmy has a new family and is a healthy, solid man who is growing in the Lord.

Many other people are in a trap like Jimmy's. They identify themselves as, "I'm John. I am an alcoholic," or "I'm Steve. I am a homosexual." Why don't we do that with other sins? I wrestle with a critical spirit at times. Why don't I say, "I'm Bob George. I am a criticizaholic"? I'll tell you why. I simply refuse to define myself by my failures. Truth is what *God* says about us. When someone accepts a label like one of these, it cements his identity in his own mind, as determined by his behavior. Therefore it is natural to assume that the behavior can never change. So people accept as inevitable and normal a bondage from which God wants to set them free.

The Two Kinds of Human Beings

How do you determine what God thinks about you? Is it really that simple? From God's point of view, there are really only two kinds of people in the world. Their identities, as always, are represented in the Bible by with whom they are identified: "For as *in Adam* all die, so *in Christ* all will be made alive" (1 Corinthians 15:22). The two kinds of people that God sees are described as being "in Adam" or "in Christ." But this is strange language to us. What does it mean to be "in" someone?

To be "in" someone means that he is our family head. As such, he has left us his name, his nature, an inheritance, and a destiny.

Let's take Adam to start with. Every human being is born into this world in Adam. That means that we are born with the same nature, inheritance, and destiny that Adam possessed since his fall. We are born spiritually dead with a sinful human nature and, unless something changes, that description will be eternal. Someone once asked a prominent Christian leader, "What does a man have to do to go to hell?" His answer was, "Absolutely nothing." Man is born headed that direction. That is the inheritance left to us by Adam.

But the inheritance left to us by Jesus Christ stands in total contrast to that of Adam:

> Consequently, just as the result of one trespass was condemnation for all men, so also the result of one act of righteousness was justification that brings life for all men. For just as through the disobedience of the one man [Adam] the many were made sinners, so also through the obedience of the one man [Christ] the many will be made righteous (Romans 5:18-19).

So therefore, the most important issue facing you and me is, With whom are we identified—with Adam or with Christ? And seeing that we are born identified with Adam and must be identified with Christ to be saved, how can our identity be changed? The subject of baptism provides the answer.

Total Identification

Since the earliest centuries of Christian history, there has been furious controversy surrounding baptism. How should it be performed? How much water should be used? This shouldn't be a surprise. Satan has always surrounded the most crucial biblical truths with confusion in an attempt to blind us to truth that will set us free.

Our confusion reminds me of when I was a boy playing ball with my dog. He was a good retriever, but he would occasionally lose sight of where the ball went. He would come back to me, tail wagging and tongue hanging out. "Rusty, over there!" I would say enthusiastically, as I pointed in the proper direction. But have you ever tried to tell a dog where to go by pointing? It never seemed to work. He would just come closer and sniff my finger. "No, no," I would say, "not my finger. Over there!" But again he would sniff my finger and give it a lick. My dog just couldn't understand the significance of what I was doing. My finger wasn't the thing I wanted him to concentrate on; it was what my finger was pointing to that was important.

We laugh at a dog's failure to understand a pointing finger, but I believe we have done the same thing with several biblical truths. Instead of catching on to what God really wants us to know, we have focused on God's symbols (pointing fingers), and even made the symbols themselves objects of contention. Baptism is one of these.

The literal meaning of baptize is to "dip" or "immerse in." The ancient Greeks used it to describe the process of dyeing. If you had a white cloth and wanted to dye it red, what would you do? You would get a vat of red dye, hold the white cloth on a stick, and "baptize" it in the dye. What happened when you pulled it out? Now you had a red cloth. It went in as one thing and came out as another, with all the characteristics of what it was baptized into.

The key meaning behind baptism is *total identification*, and that is exactly what God is trying to teach us. We are born into this world in Adam, spiritually dead, and sinners by nature. Then we hear of the good news of Jesus Christ and trust in Him as our Savior and Lord. At that instant the Holy Spirit of God baptizes us into Christ! "For we were all baptized by one Spirit into one body—and we were all given the one Spirit to drink" (1 Corinthians 12:13). This is something that happens instantaneously to every Christian at the moment of spiritual birth: *He is totally identified with Jesus Christ.*

If this has happened to you, you are no longer in Adam—you are in Christ! He is now your family head. No longer is death your inheritance: "In Christ all will be made alive" (1 Corinthians 15:22). Now you have become a "partaker of the divine nature" (2 Peter 1:4 NASB). Now heaven is your eternal destiny. Why do you have all these things? Because you are now *in Christ!*

When you stepped out of Adam into Christ, Christ stepped out of heaven into you and made you into a new creature! "Therefore, if anyone is in Christ, he is a new creation; the old has gone, the new has come!" (2 Corinthians 5:17). Being made into a new creation does not refer to your behavior; it refers to your identity.

In my case, who was I before? Bob George in Adam, without God's Spirit, spiritually dead, a guilty sinner. That man is dead and gone; he will never exist again. Who am I today? Bob George in Christ, a person who possesses the Holy Spirit, spiritually alive, and totally forgiven. Now you can be sure that this change of identity will result in some behavioral changes, but don't confuse it. Becoming a new creation refers to who I am in Christ. This is why Paul could write, "I have been crucified with Christ and I no longer live, but Christ lives in me. The life I live in the body, I live by faith in the Son of God, who loved me and gave Himself for me" (Galatians 2:20).

What Will You Do with the New You?

All over our society today—from educators, to psychologists, to Christian leaders—people are telling us that our problem is a poor self-image. Everyone needs a good self-image, they say. But the Bible tells us exactly the opposite. While the world is telling us that we need to love ourselves more, the Bible says that man's problem is that he loves himself too much! It is pride—a distorted, exaggerated view of oneself—that is the essence of sin. The Word of God says, "Do not think of yourself more highly than you ought" (Romans 12:3), and "Do nothing out of selfish ambition or vain conceit, but in humility consider others better than yourselves" (Philippians 2:3). How do you line up these verses with a world's philosophy that says, "Look out for Number One"?

No, we don't need a *good* self-image. We need a *proper* self-image—one that comes from God's Word. People say, "I'm ugly and I hate myself!" That's a contradiction in terms. If you really hated yourself, you would be *glad* you are ugly. The reason that you are angry is that you really love yourself and therefore want to be better-looking.

The Decision

As someone who has come alive in Christ, totally forgiven and accepted by Him, you now have a choice: whether you will present yourself to Him to live His life through you, or whether you will present yourself to sin and the lusts of the flesh (Romans 6:11-13).

The human soul is like a wonderfully built grand piano, a magnificent instrument. However, the quality of the music that comes from it is totally dependent upon who is at the keyboard. If a master concert pianist is at the keys, you will be carried along on the rapture of beautiful music. But let a gorilla have a shot at that piano, and the result will be chaotic noise and actual damage to the instrument. That is your daily choice.

Will you present yourself to Christ, the master pianist, who will produce the beautiful music of His life in and through you? Or will you present yourself to sin, with the discord and destruction that it produces? When Christ is controlling me, I love Bob George. When I am allowing sin to have control of me, I can't stand him. But God wants us to know and rest in who we are in Christ and to grasp the truth that we are beloved children, even in the middle of our worst failures. Only then will we have the confidence to come to Him in our time of need.

Janet's New Choice

A vivid example of the importance of identity was the story of Janet, a young woman in her late teens. She had been hospitalized for several weeks for anorexia and bulimia, a pattern of behavior that is found in overwhelmingly greater proportions among women than among men. An anorexic person thinks she is fat and becomes obsessed with losing weight. She starves herself and becomes deceived into thinking she is still fat, even when she has gotten to the point of looking like a living skeleton. The bulimic part of the behavior is the pattern of losing control of the diet. The person gorges herself, feels guilty about it, then forces herself to vomit the food to keep from gaining weight. This is what Janet was into.

For six solid weeks, she had been getting treatment in one of the leading hospitals in Dallas. But those treating her did not consult what God has to say about human nature. They said she had a "poor self-image" that needed improvement. Therefore they had her practicing Hindu meditation techniques which involved "catching the sunlight and bringing it into your body" to bring about healing, strength, and self-confidence. (And there are those who say you have to "put your brain in neutral" to be a Christian!) It reminds me of what God said, "Although they claimed to be wise, they became fools" (Romans 1:22).

After six weeks of failure, her parents brought her to me. I told them, "Leave her here for a few days. We'll let her do some volunteer work around the office, and I'll counsel with her." Less than a week later, Janet went home, totally freed of her self-destructive behavior. How? Not because I am some supercounselor. It is because truth sets you free. The counselors in the hospital did not consult truth. I used the Word of God. In particular, the Bible revealed the premise that the hospital counselors held in error. Janet's problem, which is the problem of every person in this camp, was not a poor self-image. It was a total, obsessive preoccupation with herself. The answer was not a "positive" self-image. It was a *proper* self-image, based on truth.

Janet and I dug into the Word of God together. Quickly we identified that she was a typical Christian—she knew she was going to heaven when she died, but she had no idea how God loves and accepts her today, nor did she know about the life of Christ in her. Without a solid foundation for determining her identity in Christ, she was forced to go to the world to determine it. And what does the world say? Just watch television: If you want to be admired by members of your own sex and desired by members of the opposite sex, you need to look like the models in the ads. If there is an ounce of fat on you, forget it. You'll be a nobody, and nobody will ever want you.

Janet bought this garbage. Many other people have, too. It's a lie, but Janet became obsessed with trying to obtain the acceptance that the world offered—acceptance that is always offered with a string attached. It's always, "I'll love you *if...*" "I'll accept you *if...*" That string always leads to bondage. Janet and I talked about this error and looked into the Bible to discover what God says about her. She was amazed, and she responded immediately with joy and gratitude to Christ.

> "It's like saying to God, 'God, You don't know what You're doing. You can create a world, all right, but You really blew it when You made me.'"

Then we attacked the problem of her behavior. "Janet," I said, "what does God say about you?"

"He says I'm holy and perfectly loved by Him."

"For how long?" I asked.

"Forever."

"Do you think God knew what He was doing when He made you? Do you think He could have made you differently if He wanted to?"

"Sure," she said.

"Then how much sense does it make for you to sit around all day thinking about what's imperfect about you? To be thinking constantly about how much you weigh? Just to be thinking about yourself all day long every day? It's like saying to God, 'God, You don't know what You're doing. You can create a world, all right, but You really blew it when You made me.'"

Janet thought a while. "It's really pretty dumb, isn't it?"

I nodded. "Janet, no man is going to love you because you are as thin as a rake. Someone is going to love you because of the person you are. If someone accepts you or rejects you because of your waistline, then his love isn't worth anything at all. It isn't even love.

"Being preoccupied with yourself just makes you miserable. Jesus said, 'I didn't come to be served, but to serve.' We never find happiness by thinking about ourselves all the time. We discover real meaning and purpose in life when we learn to be thinking about others, when we are learning to serve other people. You're a butterfly, Janet!" She gave me a big smile. "Get up and fly!"

This is just an excerpt. It wasn't a magical, instantaneous counseling session. But Janet did truly go free, and the answer was seeing that she was a holy, loved child of God. That identity is a truth that the opinions of other people cannot affect. When she became dependent on Christ, who loved her and lived in her, she became free from her terrible bondage.

⸺⸻⸺

The believer's identity in Christ is not a side issue; it is central to experiencing the real Christian life. If we do not have a firm grip on this issue, we will not have the confidence to go to our God and Father for help when we need it the most. But if we'll take a lesson from a little boy named John-John and rest in who we are, we can go boldly to the throne of grace and begin to discover the riches and freedom that we already have in Christ because we are children of the King!

7

LOVED *AND* ACCEPTED

My son, Bobby, had just graduated from college and was involved in the hard process of finding that first job. The job situation in Dallas at the time was extremely difficult. The economy was down, and even very experienced businessmen were scrambling. Many people were out of work. Obviously, a young man, fresh out of college, wasn't in the best of positions. Seeing that he was discouraged, I invited him to get together for breakfast to see if I could offer some encouragement and advice.

We had a long, profitable discussion about work, the business world, and interviewing, and he did seem to be perking up. We went on to talk about other things and enjoyed a good time of just being together. As our conversation was winding down, Bobby said, "Dad, thanks a lot for your time. I really was getting down on myself, but you've helped a lot.

"You know," he said, "one thing I've always known is that you love me. I've never doubted it. You've shown me that in all kinds of ways." I was naturally pleased to hear that, but somehow, it didn't seem complete. I pondered for a few seconds, then God seemed to put a new thought in my mind.

"Bobby, I really do love you—always have and always will—but let me ask you this question. Have you always known that I *accept* you?"

Bobby seemed taken aback. He asked, "What do you mean?"

"I mean there's a difference between love and acceptance. You say you're confident that I love you, but acceptance is something else. Do you know, for example, that I accept you just like you are? That I really like *you*?"

Bobby thought a few moments. Then, in a serious tone, he said, "No, Dad, I guess I really don't. I don't think I have really felt that you accept me." I asked him to tell me about it.

He continued. "I guess I always felt that you would like it if I was more spiritual. You know, if I read my Bible more, or did more Christian activities, or maybe went into full-time Christian work like you did, instead of going into business."

As Bobby shared his true feelings, it stirred up many convicting memories in me. I thought back to the early days of my conversion. Bobby and my daughter, Debbie, were about eight and ten years old, and I soon had led them to know Jesus Christ as their Savior. I am very thankful to have had the experience, but at the time, I was only able to share what I knew myself: I was very strong in stating that Jesus Christ had died on the cross for the forgiveness of our sins, but I was very weak on the fact that He came to live in and through us. You can only take someone else as far as you have come.

Being an extremely gung-ho new Christian, I became heavily involved in personal evangelism. I was very proud of being a "bold witness for Christ." I was sometimes immature and awkward, but my zeal was genuine. Unfortunately, though, I began to consider my lifestyle as the standard other people should live up to. I pressured many people, using subtle and not-so-subtle guilt trips to get them to be like me. I did the same thing to my children. Bobby would come in and announce that he had met a new kid on the block and had been having fun playing with him. I would look him in the eye and ask, "That's good, Bobby. Did you witness to him?" I expected my nine-year-old son to share an evangelistic message with his friend within 15 minutes of meeting him.

One of the worst and most embarrassing episodes took place a couple of years later. I was by this time in full-time ministry and was attending a training conference. One of the speakers, who had a tremendous reputation as an effective witness, talked about how he had taken his children out to share Christ door-to-door. When I saw all the positive attention he was getting, I thought to myself, "I can do that, too!" After all, I was a bold witness. I wasn't afraid to go knocking on strangers' doors to share my faith! So there I was, with my shy, sensitive, eleven-year-old son, walking through neighborhoods sharing Christ with strangers—all to impress other Christians, just so I could receive some of the same accolades that the other man received—while poor Bobby was being scared out of his socks.

I asked Bobby if he remembered that occasion. He remembered it vividly, and admitted that way back then he had determined in his own mind that if that's what it takes to be a good Christian, he would stay out on the periphery and not get too deeply involved. Then, believing in his heart that he wasn't living up to my standards for acceptance, believing that I disapproved of him, he became more and more reserved and distant from me. I could have told him 10,000 times how much I loved him. I could have given him thousands of hugs and kisses, hundreds of gifts. And yet all these demonstrations of my love would have fallen meaningless on deaf ears—*because he didn't believe that I accepted him.*

I finally had the chance to tell him that I was wrong, and to ask Bobby to forgive me for my foolishness through the years. Most importantly, I had the chance to tell him that I not only loved him and always would, but that I accepted him just as he was and that he never had to do or become anything else to earn my acceptance. There was no "if" attached to my acceptance of him at all. I just plain accepted and liked him right now. Our relationship began anew that morning. I also learned a valuable insight: *Love becomes practically meaningless apart from acceptance.*

Do You Believe that God *Accepts* You?

I have since discovered that many Christians are relating to God much as Bobby related to me. Most of them can quote John 3:16: "For God so loved the world..." Yet, they walk around every day feeling that God is sick to His stomach over them because of their failure to live up to His standards. Often, though, it's not even God's standards that they are trying to keep, but regulations imposed by themselves or other people.

There is a certain mind-set that is especially destructive, called the "Phantom Christian." The Phantom Christian is that imaginary person that many of us are continually comparing ourselves to. He is the super-spiritual man who gets up every day at 4:00 a.m. so he can pray for four hours. Then he reads his Bible for four hours. He goes to work (at which he is tops in his field), where he effectively shares Christ with everyone in his office. He teaches several Bible studies, goes to church every time the doors are open, and serves on several committees. He is also a wonderful spiritual leader at home—a sterling example of a loving husband and father, who leads stimulating family devotions every day for his "Proverbs 31" wife and perfect children.

Of course no one could live up to such a standard. Even if some person had the ability, he would still need 100 hours in a day! Rationally, we all know that the Phantom Christian is ridiculous, but the problem is that he is never brought to our consciousness. He is a vague ghost that sits in the back of our minds, creating a sense of failure to measure up. That is the reason why many, many Christians live under continual guilt. For those who believe that the Phantom Christian is God's standard for acceptance, God seems a million miles away, sitting in heaven with His arms folded in disapproval. They don't bother offering prayers because they know He would never answer them.

People in this bondage know well the biblical teaching that God loves them, but they clearly do not believe in their hearts that God *accepts* them. And apart from knowing about and resting in God's acceptance, His love becomes practically meaningless and irrelevant in daily living. I have often talked of God's love in counseling appointments and seen Christians react bitterly to the words. "So what?" they say. "He loves everybody!" What they are saying is that the only love they understand coming from God is some kind of vague, universal, impersonal love.

Ignorance...or Worse?

In many cases, God's true acceptance of us in Christ and the inheritance we have in Him simply isn't taught. However, ignorance of the Word of God is not the only reason for this condition. Many people who know the Bible intimately experience the same thing. I was speaking to the student body of a seminary one time. In the course of discussing the Christian's identity in Christ, I asked a series of questions. "How many of you," I asked, "are as righteous and acceptable *in the sight of God* as I am?" Every hand in the auditorium was raised. "How many of you," I asked again, "are as righteous and acceptable *in the sight of God* as Billy Graham?" This time about half of the audience raised their hands. "How many of you are as acceptable and righteous *in the sight of God* as the apostle Paul?" There were around 10 percent of the hands raised. "Now here's the really tough one," I said. "How many of you *in the sight of God* are as righteous and acceptable as *Jesus Christ?*" Only three hands were raised out of an entire auditorium of seminary students.

Mind you, this was not a case of ignorance. These men were attending a fine seminary. Every person in that audience could have defended aggressively the doctrine of justification by faith. They had the truth in their *heads*, all right. But did they have the truth in their *hearts?* It is a perfect illustration of the principle that a person can know what the Bible *says* but not necessarily know what it *means.* I wonder: Would *you* have raised your hand?

> You should have seen some of their faces! I think some of them feared that lightning would strike me on the spot!

I finally told that group of students the same incredible truth that I am laying before you. "I'm going to say this to you straightforward, so there's no chance you'll miss it," I began. *"If you are a true Christian, then you are as righteous and acceptable in the sight of God as Jesus Christ!"* You should have seen some of their faces! I think some of them feared that lightning would strike me on the spot!

What's your reaction? If you are as shocked as many of those students were, then it may be that you just don't know who you are in Christ. It may be that you know a great deal of doctrine, but your daily Christian life is still more a burden than a blessing. You may have tried and tried to change your life without success, in spite of all the seminars, books, and Web sites you have searched. Whatever your situation, I have great news to share with you. Let's look at some of the fantastic inheritance that we have received in Jesus Christ. It's my prayer that you will never again wrestle with doubts about God's acceptance of you, so that you can go on to discover the immeasurable wonders of His love.

The Free Gift

Most Christians, I find, understand the general idea behind forgiveness:

God took our sins and gave them to Jesus. But that's only half the message! God also took Christ's perfect righteousness and gave it to us! Second Corinthians 5:21 says, "God made Him who had no sin to be sin for us, so that *in Him we might become the righteousness of God.*" How could I stand up and declare that *in the sight of God* I am as righteous and acceptable as Jesus Christ? Because of what I *do*? No way! It's because of *who I am* in Christ.

The Bible goes to great lengths to declare that righteousness is a free gift that a man receives by faith. Romans 5:17 is explicit:

> For if, by the trespass of the one man [Adam], death reigned through that one man, how much more will those who receive God's abundant provision of grace and of the *gift of righteousness* reign in life through the one man, Jesus Christ.

Righteousness (a right standing of total acceptability before God) is a *gift*. You don't work for it. You don't earn it. You don't deserve it. Like any gift, all you can do is accept it or reject it. And once you have it, it's yours.

People often respond to me, "I just can't conceive of how God can make me righteous." I reply, "I've got a better question. How could God make Jesus become sin?" Honestly, I have much less trouble understanding how God could make me righteous than I do trying to understand how God could make His perfect Son become sin. But 2 Corinthians 5:21 teaches both.

Those seminary students, able to effectively defend the doctrine of justification by faith, were too timid to state in so many words that they are as righteous as Jesus. And yet to say one is to say the other. The word *justified means* to be "declared totally righteous." What hinders someone who knows what the Bible teaches on justification from actually applying it is the attitude that our righteousness in Christ is dealing only with where we go when we die, and that here and now our acceptance is based on our performance. As long as someone thinks this way, he will experience no practical benefit at all from knowing that he is justified in Christ. He will continue dealing with God as if on a merit system, and he will experience the same kind of emotional barrier between himself and God (even though there's no barrier from God's perspective) that my son, Bobby, felt with me. The truth is that God sees us as totally acceptable and righteous in His sight *right now*—not because of what we do, but because of what Christ has done for us.

Praying on the Basis of Your Total Acceptability

The first application where we will discover whether or not we really believe this is prayer. How do we approach God? How we pray reveals our perception of God's acceptance and what we think He desires from us. What God wants is for us to *trust* Him and His Word—the Word that tells us that Christ has done it all—and to *act* on it by approaching "the throne of grace with *confidence*, so that we may receive mercy and find grace to help in our time of need" (Hebrews 4:16).

Notice that God said, "in our time of need." What is your greatest time of need? Isn't it when you are failing, experiencing temptation, or in the grip of some sin? But if you don't trust that you have been made totally acceptable in God's sight, you will never have the boldness to approach Him. You will linger outside His throne room, trying to find a way to get "worthy" enough to go in. The end result is that you will avoid going to your only source of help (God) when you need Him the most! When could you or I ever be "worthy" to enter the throne room of a holy God on our own? Never. But the New Testament continually and strongly urges us to take full advantage in prayer of what God has done through Christ, "in whom we have *boldness* and *confident access* through faith in Him" (Ephesians 3:12 NASB). Where do we get boldness and confidence? "Through faith in Him." It's all tied up in the phrase to pray "in Jesus' name."

I often ask groups, "What does it mean to pray in Jesus' name?" We've heard the phrase uncounted times. We all end our prayers with it. But nobody seems to know why. Probably the most honest answer I have heard is, "It's a way to end our prayers, like 'Roger, over and out.'" No, it's much more than just a way to end our prayers. To pray in Jesus' name means that we are recognizing two things. First, we are recognizing that *apart from Him* there is no way that we could be accepted by a holy God. But second, we are declaring that *because of Him* and what He has done we can go *boldly* to God *at any time* with full confidence that we will find open, accepting arms! Not because of our own righteousness—because we don't have any—but in *His*. Galatians 3:27 says, "For all of you who were baptized into Christ have *clothed yourselves with Christ*." Because we are *in Him* we are totally acceptable to God!

Now realize that I am talking about *ourselves* being acceptable to God, not necessarily our *actions*. In my identity I am eternally acceptable to Him, but that doesn't mean that everything I *do* is all right. He may put His arm around me, so to speak, and show me the truth about something in my life that is out of line: an attitude, action, or habit. Why? So He can *change* my attitude that is out of line, resulting in a change of action. But at no time is His acceptance of *me* ever in question. At no time does He ever deal with me except in perfect love, acceptance, wisdom, and kindness. Because I am a child of God, there is no occasion in life when He would not attend to my prayer that is offered in faith—that is, in Jesus' name!

Prayer becomes the key initial application of our identity in Christ because it is inescapable. The Bible says to "pray continually" (1 Thessalonians 5:17), and I find that is exactly the heart's desire of someone in whom Christ lives and who is experiencing His love and acceptance. But the moment we are moved to approach God in prayer, the extent to which we trust in His acceptance comes immediately into play. How confident are we that His ears are open to us? I don't believe that very many Christians have much assurance in prayer. And it's because we don't know who we are.

The Most Life-Changing Power in the Universe

Based on my experience in teaching and counseling thousands of people, I have come to believe that the most destructive force in human experience is living under *conditional love and acceptance*. That is, "I love you *if*..." This is true on a purely natural level. People who grow up in a home where their parents' love and acceptance had to be earned go on to endure pain and struggle for a lifetime. On the other hand, those who grow up in an environment where there is love and acceptance without conditions usually have a more confident and positive outlook as they attack life. But this is, again, just speaking on a natural level.

The same principle is true and is magnified in regard to a person's spiritual life. Have you ever wondered why the history of religion is so sordid? Have you ever noticed that religious people can be the meanest people on earth? It's because religion *makes* people mean! All forms of religion—man's attempt *to reach up to God*—are based on trying to earn the acceptance and response of God, or "the gods." Only Christianity, pure and undiluted, speaks of a loving and accepting God *who reached down to man* to offer forgiveness and life!

If the most destructive force in human experience is conditional love and acceptance, it is also true that the most powerful, life-changing power in existence is the message of God's unconditional love and acceptance in Jesus Christ. An unforgettable example is the story of Jean.

Jean's Encounter with God's Love and Acceptance

Jean had struggled all of her adult life. Married to a career military man who was driven by ambition, she lived in many parts of the world. However, rather than enjoying an exciting lifestyle, Jean was plagued by continual depression. She barely hung on through her dependency upon medically prescribed drugs. But often even they could not give her comfort against the onslaught of depression. On four separate occasions, the emotional pain drove Jean to attempt to take her own life. On her last attempt, she lingered between life and death in a coma for four days. Her husband, tired of the burden of putting up with her, deserted and divorced her.

After her fourth attempt at suicide, she was too frightened to try again. She resigned herself to living, but the depression continued. Alone, Jean returned to the United States to try to establish some kind of life. Here in Dallas, she was invited to a home Bible study that I was teaching. She immediately responded with joy to the good news and received Jesus Christ. Jean was amazed as she began to discover what God said about her in the Scriptures. She hung on every verse that talked of God's love and acceptance of her and of her new identity in Christ. Her depressed appearance, tight nervousness, and labored movements began to be replaced by smiling bright eyes, calm relaxation, and a spring in her step. Jean's total preoccupation with herself was replaced by a genuine concern for other people. Soon the depression was only a memory.

I'll never forget the day Jean said to me with a beaming countenance, "Bob, all my life I've tried to kill myself—*and I finally succeeded!*" It was more than a little jarring. She laughed at my expression and explained, "I was so unhappy for so long. But now I have learned how much God loves me, and I'm learning more every day. That old Jean is dead and gone. She died at the cross with Jesus. But the new Jean is alive and perfectly loved in Him."

> "Since I quit *trying* to get people to love me, I have found more love than I could ever measure in God's other children."

She went on to explain. "All my life I looked for someone to love me and to accept me just like I am. I tried to earn my family's acceptance. I tried to earn my husband's acceptance. I tried to earn my children's love. I tried to earn my friends' love. And all along I was trying to earn God's love and acceptance. But it's terribly hard to make other people love you when you think you're unlovable. Only in Jesus have I found love and acceptance that I can count on forever. But the wonderful thing is that since I quit *trying* to get people to love me, I have found more love than I could ever measure in God's other children."

More than five years have passed since I first met Jean. She has been absolutely free from depression every one of those five years. She is today a joyful, delightful Christian, full of compassion and love. She is a fine, sensitive, and wise counselor to other people who are in the same trap of depression and despair that she escaped through Christ.

⟶

Jesus said, "I am the bread of life; he who comes to Me will not hunger, and he who believes in Me will never thirst" (John 6:35 NASB). Every human being born into this poor, sin-sick world is born with a craving for unconditional love and acceptance. When we learn to rely totally on Jesus Christ, we find Him to be just what He promised: the total satisfaction for that gnawing hunger and thirst. In Him we find unconditional love, unconditional acceptance, and meaning and purpose in life. All searching comes to an end in Him.

8

THE GREAT EXCHANGE

One of the greatest illustrations to me of the importance of spiritual knowledge is the true story of a man named Ira Yates. During the 1920s, Mr. Yates owned a great deal of land in west Texas upon which he raised sheep. The land was poor, and he struggled to get ahead financially. Eventually he came up with the notion of getting an oil company to drill on his ranch, even though everyone considered the land worthless.

When the oil company began drilling at a very shallow depth they struck the largest oil deposit at that time to be found on the North American continent—a deposit that produced over 80,000 barrels of oil every day! Overnight, Mr. Yates became a multimillionaire! Or did he? No, if you think about it, Mr. Yates had been a multimillionaire ever since he had first acquired the land. The oil had always been there. Mr. Yates just didn't know it.

This is a picture of many Christians today. The Bible tells us that God "has blessed us in the heavenly realms with every spiritual blessing in Christ" (Ephesians 1:3). But like Mr. Yates, most of us are unaware of the incredible riches that we *already have* in Christ. So we live in spiritual poverty.

As I said previously, many Christians today have an understanding

of salvation that is not necessarily *wrong*, but much *too small*. It's for this
same reason that Paul, in his letter to the Ephesians, prayed for them

> that the God of our Lord Jesus Christ, the Father of glory, may
> give to you a spirit of wisdom and of revelation in the knowl-
> edge of Him. I pray that *the eyes of your heart may be enlightened,*
> so that you may know what is the hope of His calling, what
> are the riches of the glory of His inheritance in the saints, and
> what is the surpassing greatness of His power toward us who
> believe (Ephesians 1:17-19 NASB).

These are the same things that Paul was referring to in 1 Corinthians
2:9 where he said, "No eye has seen, no ear has heard, no mind has
conceived what God has prepared for those who love Him." How desperately we need this knowledge! But when he talks of "the eyes of our
hearts" being opened, it's obvious that the apostle is referring to something deeper than our intellect, something that God Himself must give
us power to understand. He is talking about a true *heart* knowledge
of Him and His love. Therefore we must approach God's truth with a
humble, teachable, dependent attitude. This knowledge doesn't come
through our own intelligence and effort alone: "God has revealed it to
us by His Spirit" (1 Corinthians 2:10). Though I didn't know it at the
time, this is what I was really praying for myself in those days that I
was driving down the expressway with tears streaming down my cheeks.
When I say these truths are life-changing, I am speaking from personal
experience. My life has been changed.

The same thing is true when I speak of the difference between head
knowledge and heart knowledge of the Word of God. It is an amazing
experience for me to go back and listen to old tapes of myself teaching.
Back then I taught most of the same truths, using the same verses I do
today. But I can tell you for a fact that in my heart I didn't understand
what I was talking about. But today my experience of God's love and
acceptance is so real that I can't describe it. That's why Paul's prayer for
the Ephesians is my prayer for you. That as we explore more of our inheritance, you will have your eyes opened to understand with your heart as
well as your mind "what God has freely given us" (1 Corinthians 2:12)
through Jesus Christ!

The Riches of Our Total Acceptance by God

What is our inheritance in Christ? And how does knowing this translate into a changed life? In answer, let's begin with the major principle that ties it all together: *You will never have a* changed *life until you experience the* exchanged *life.*

Christians are continually trying to *change* their lives; but God is calling us to experience the *exchanged* life. Christianity is not a self-improvement program. It isn't a reformation project. It is resurrection! It is new life! And it is expressed in terms of a total exchange of identity. Jesus Christ identified Himself with us in our death in order that we might be identified with Him in His resurrection. We give Christ all that we were—spiritually dead, guilty sinners—and Christ gives us all that He is—resurrected life, forgiveness, righteousness, acceptance.

We have total acceptance because we have experienced a total exchange: "God made Him who had no sin to be sin for us, so that in Him we might become the righteousness of God" (2 Corinthians 5:21). We looked at this truth in the last chapter. Let's go on now to examine some of the *results* of our being given a standing of total acceptance before God (our justification).

We Have Been Made at Peace with God

"Therefore, since we have been justified through faith, we have peace with God through our Lord Jesus Christ" (Romans 5:1). This verse isn't referring to a feeling, such as the "peace *of* God"; it is talking about the kind of peace which is the opposite of war. The book of Romans begins with a discussion of the wrath of God against the human race because of sin (Romans 1:18). Now, having explained the good news, Paul declares that we have peace with God—no more hostility or division. We have been totally reconciled to Him once and for all.

We Are Safe from God's Wrath

"Since we have now been justified by His blood, how much more shall we be saved from God's wrath through Him!" (Romans 5:9). How can we be sure that God will not deal with us in anger because of our sins? Because Christ took all of God's anger upon Himself at the cross, and we are now in Him, hidden within His righteousness.

It has always hit me as very strange that in many Christian groups the good news of Jesus Christ seems to be reserved for the lost man, while Christians are living in guilt, insecurity, and fear of God's anger. You could be an ax murderer or a Mafia hit man, and the message will be, "God loves you, and Jesus Christ died for your sins. All you need to do is receive Him by faith and you'll be saved!" That's right! Any man who comes to Jesus Christ will be saved, regardless of his past. However, the believers are getting a message like this: "You dirty, rotten backsliders! You'd better clean up your act, or God's punishment will fall on you!" First you get the good news, then after you're a Christian you get the bad news.

Romans 5:6-10 is trying to answer this very error. Paraphrased, it says: If God demonstrated the greatness of His love toward you in that—even when you were helpless, ungodly sinners, and His enemies—Christ died for you, *how much more*—now that you are members of the family!—are you secure from fear of His judgment!

We Have Been Freed from All Fear of Condemnation

"Therefore, there is now no condemnation [judgment, punishment] for those who are in Christ Jesus" (Romans 8:1). This verse is as crystal clear as it can be. A Christian (one who is "in Christ Jesus") will never face judgment for his sins. How can we be sure? Again, because Christ took our judgment upon Himself and there is none left for us. We are now *in Him*, having received His righteousness.

We Have Been Made Perfect Forever

By one sacrifice He has made perfect forever those who are being made holy" (Hebrews 10:14). I often help people walk through this verse phrase by phrase so they will receive the full impact of it. Just recently I concluded a radio conversation with Karen, a young woman who had lived for years with guilt feelings. After reading Hebrews 10:14, I quizzed her.

"Karen, what did that verse say about you?" I asked.

"I've been made perfect," Karen answered.

"For how long have you been made perfect?"

"Forever," she answered.

"How did you become perfect, Karen," I continued. "Is it because you *act* perfect?"

"No," she said. She hesitated in thought for a moment. "It says, 'by one sacrifice.' It's because of what Jesus did for us."

"Then Karen, if this is true (and the Bible says it is), how does it make you feel?"

"Happy...free. It makes me want to get to know God better. It makes me want to love Him more." Karen got the message.

Many people wonder why they find it hard to love God, even though they believe they should. The answer is very simple and is explained in 1 John 4:10,18-19:

> This is love: *not that we loved God, but that He loved us* and sent His Son as the one who would turn aside His wrath, taking away our sins...There is no fear in love. But perfect love drives out fear, because fear has to do with punishment. The man who fears is not made perfect in love. *We love because He first loved us.*

A dear friend of mine, Bonnie, had been suicidal due to years of abject depression. She had worked herself to the point of exhaustion, trying to be "good enough" to be accepted by God. Then she heard of God's acceptance in Christ and of her new identity in Him. She said, "I tried and tried to love God. I was taught I was *supposed* to love Him, and I felt that I *should* love Him. But I found that I couldn't. It just wasn't in me. Finally I discovered *how God loved me*, and the struggle to love Him ended. From then on, loving God became the most natural thing in the world."

> The New Testament is so blatant and bold in its proclamations of who we are in Christ that it boggles the mind...Don't water it down!

We must *receive* God's love and *rest* in His total acceptance before we will ever be able to return it. The more we learn about and experience God's love on a daily basis, the more we will find ourselves responding with love for Him and love for other people.

The New Testament is so blatant and bold in its proclamations of who we are in Christ that it boggles the mind. It's no wonder that we find it so hard to believe. Many people find it necessary to water it down and resist the message by saying, "What the Bible *really* means here is..." But don't water it down! *The Bible really means exactly what it says!* We *have* been made perfect. In our own eyes? No. According to our behavior? No. We have been made perfectly acceptable in *God's* eyes.

We have difficulty with this simply because we persist in living by sight rather than by faith. What is faith? The Bible tells us: "Now faith is being sure of what we hope for and certain of what we *do not see*" (Hebrews 11:1). If we could see these things, we wouldn't need faith at all. Faith is hearing a promise of God and acting on it, regardless of what we see.

We Have Been Made Complete

"For in Him [Christ] all the fullness of Deity dwells in bodily form, and in Him you have been made complete"(Colossians 2:9-10 NASB). Can you add to completeness? No. You can't get any "completer."

There were apple trees all over the area of Indiana where I grew up. We kids used to get those apples when they were still immature—small and hard as rocks—and have fights with them. I had a great feeling of accomplishment when I could really clock one of my buddies in the head with one. Now were those apples perfect in nature? Yes, absolutely. Everything that would ever be in them was already there. But were they *mature*? No.

We Christians have been made complete in Christ. We are forgiven, redeemed, made spiritually alive, and we stand in the righteousness of Christ, totally accepted. Are we perfectly mature? No. That won't happen until the day of resurrection, when we receive new bodies to go with the resurrected spirits we already possess.

God has a lot of building and training to do in us yet. We ought to see each other with an invisible sign on our chests reading, "Under construction." It would make us more tolerant and forgiving toward one another. Until then, we can be sure that God "who began a good work in you will carry it on to completion until the day of Christ Jesus" (Philippians 1:6). Even though we are aware of the sometimes-difficult process of growth,

He sees us as already there. As I said to a radio listener, "God will never love or accept you one ounce less or one ounce more than He does *right this minute*." That's a truth to build a life on!

We Have Been Made Citizens of Heaven

"But our citizenship is in heaven. And we eagerly await a Savior from there, the Lord Jesus Christ" (Philippians 3:20). My wife's story illustrates a tremendous application of this truth. Amy was born in Russia and lived in Germany after the war. While in the army, I married her and brought her to the United States. As an American citizen today, she has no relation whatsoever to the Communist doctrine she heard as a child. She has full citizenship in a different country. She has a new identity.

Let's say, though, that some Russian agents were following her around, saying, "You're Russian. You have to do what we tell you. You can't change who you are. You work for us." There's no reason to waste time arguing with them. Amy could just rely on the truth. "Get lost. I don't have any relation to you anymore. My identity is no longer Russian. I am an American citizen! I'm subject to the rights, privileges, and laws of the United States of America. Get out of here or I'll call the police!"

That's how we are to deal with the lies of the devil. We all know the experience of wanting to be everything God wants us to be, and yet failing. We know the whispering voice in our ear: "You'll never make it. You're a miserable Christian. God has forsaken you. You're totally unacceptable." Don't waste time and effort arguing with him. Just reject the lie and fall back on who God says you are! "I am a child of God. If you don't like something about me, Satan, take it up with Jesus. He's my Lord. I have no relation to you at all."

Amy can say, "I am dead to Russia, and alive to the United States." In the same way, we can say, "I am dead to sin and to the wages of it, and alive to God." Romans 6:3-4 says:

> Or do you not know that all of us who have been baptized into Christ Jesus have been baptized into His death? Therefore we have been buried with Him through baptism into death, so that as Christ was raised from the dead through the glory of the Father, so we too might walk in newness of life (NASB).

Because we have experienced God's great exchange, we can consider the past dead and gone, and concentrate on walking in the new life we have received.

Here-and-Now Life and Power

Paul wrote, "I am not ashamed of the gospel, because it is the *power of God* for the salvation of everyone who believes" (Romans 1:16). It is a message of love, of acceptance, of life. Not only so that we can go to heaven when we die. It is *life*, and *power* for living here and now:

> I have been crucified with Christ and I no longer live, but *Christ lives in me*. The life I live in the body, I live by *faith* in the Son of God who loved me and gave Himself for me (Galatians 2:20).

There are many people who find this message offensive and get angry. There's another group which says, "Yes, yes, I know what you're saying is true. But you can't just camp on these things. You have to go on to practical truth." Listen! There is *nothing* more practical than the message of God's love and grace, and the believer's identity in Christ! People are always looking for God's power, and this is it!

The Practical Power of New Identity

As proof, let's take a really tough situation. How would you counsel someone who is caught up in homosexuality? Does Jesus Christ have an answer for him? We all know it's wrong. The world can call it a "sickness," an "alternative lifestyle," or a "sexual preference." But nobody who accepts the Bible as the Word of God can call it anything but sin. But accepting that it is sin, just proving that it's wrong, is not an answer. What answer can we offer a man caught in this terrible bondage? I know of only one: He needs not just a change of *behavior* but a totally new *identity*.

Lee slumped in a chair in my office as he told his story. "I have been a homosexual for many years," he said. He spoke in a low voice. He was visibly depressed and tired. "Then just a few months ago, I was introduced to Jesus Christ by some friends. I started attending church, and I thought everything had changed. But now there's a guy in church that I'm attracted to, and I can't get him out of my mind."

Lee's voice broke with emotion as he told of his heartache, of how, in spite of his efforts to change, he found himself falling back into the same old habits.

"Let's back up for a moment," I began, "and let me discuss what salvation is all about." I explained the gospel, about Jesus Christ's death for us to deal with the sin issue, and His resurrection, by which He can now give us His very life. I covered that salvation is not our changing our own lives; it is God making us into a new creation. My first goal was to discover if Lee was truly a Christian.

Based on his answers, he was truly born again. He had indeed received Christ, so our work had to be done elsewhere. What do you do if you're a Christian and you are wrestling with temptations and desires that are obviously sinful? In Lee's case, as in most counseling situations like this, there were some issues that needed to be clarified.

"Lee," I said, "when you received Christ, what part of you was born again?"

He thought for a moment. "I guess, my spirit."

"That's right," I answered. "When we are saved, our *bodies* aren't born again. I've got the same one I had before and, in fact, it's getting worse. And neither are our *souls* (our mind, emotions, and will) born again. In other words, you and I can think the same dumb thoughts, have the same ungodly desires, and do the same sinful things as we could before we became Christians. That's why the Bible says, 'Do not conform any longer to the pattern of this world, but be transformed by the *renewing of your mind*' (Romans 12:2). We used to live in total darkness, at the mercy of the lies of Satan, but now we can be set free by truth. The Spirit of God lives in you, and He wants to renew your mind. And Jesus promised 'the truth will set you free.' But the 'renewing of your mind' is a lifelong *process*."

Living in Accord with Who We Are

I went on to talk with Lee about truth in many areas, beginning with the issue of identity. Who did Lee say he was in the beginning of our conversation? "I am a homosexual." But is that true? Is that who *God* says he is? I began by turning to 1 Corinthians 6:9-10 and we read:

Do you not know that the wicked will not inherit the kingdom
of God? Do not be deceived: Neither the sexually immoral nor
idolators nor adulterers nor male prostitutes nor homosexual
offenders nor thieves nor the greedy nor drunkards nor slander-
ers nor swindlers will inherit the kingdom of God.

Wow, that's tough! Why start there? Because I'm committed to truth.
And according to God's Word, I have to call homosexuality what God
calls it—sin. But before anyone begins feeling self-righteous, let me also
point out that in the same list are things like "greedy" and "slander-
ers." How many of us can say that we are totally free from all covetous
desires? How many of us can say that we never gossip? If it weren't for
the matchless grace of God in Jesus Christ, those sins—just as much
as homosexuality—would be enough to condemn us to hell.

Too often, we stop reading the Bible in the wrong place. Lee really
didn't need convincing—he knew his sins. What he needed was good
news that would set him free! And it's right there in the next verse: "And
that is what some of you *were*" (1 Corinthians 6:11).

"Do you see that, Lee?" I asked. "You came in here and told me that
you are a homosexual. But the Bible says that that's what you *were*. That's
not your identity today! Let me finish reading the verse: 'But *you were
washed, you were sanctified, you were justified* in the name of the Lord
Jesus Christ and by the Spirit of our God'" (1 Corinthians 6:11). I went
on to explain. "When God looks at you, He doesn't see a person with the
identity 'homosexual.' You are a child of God, Lee! That's who you *are*."
We went on to study many more Scriptures that talk of the believer's
identity in Christ.

After much time in study and discussion, Lee responded this way:
"Bob, if these things are really who I am, then that old activity just doesn't
make any sense, does it?" That's exactly the point. You see, if a person's
identity is "homosexual," then homosexual activity is the only natural
and logical thing you can expect. But if a person's identity is "child of
God"—holy, beloved, righteous in God's sight—then that old behavior
makes no sense at all. It is totally inconsistent with who you are! Lee
caught that truth, and it was the beginning of his turnaround.

A Way of Life that Makes Sense

There was more, of course. In the remainder of 1 Corinthians 6 it discusses reasonable, logical behavior that should result from the truth of who you are in verse 11:

> Do you not know that your bodies are members of Christ Himself? Shall I then take the members of Christ and unite them with a prostitute? Never! Do you not know that he who unites himself with a prostitute is one with her in body?...But he who unites himself with the Lord is one with Him in spirit. Flee from sexual immorality...Do you not know that your body is a temple of the Holy Spirit, who is in you, whom you have received from God? You are not your own; you were bought at a price. Therefore honor God with your body (1 Corinthians 6:15-20).

The recurring phrase "Do you not know?" hammers home the truth that if you know who you are *in Christ*, then it makes no sense to do anything else but to offer yourself to God for His use.

"When we're choosing a lie, we are all saying the same thing as Adam: 'God, You don't know what You're talking about. This other thing is more fun than what You say.'"

Beginning with this foundation, we worked hard to identify principles of truth and error that would enable Lee to escape temptation. "The first sin of Adam and Eve," I explained, "was their decision to deny God as the only source of truth, and to determine for themselves good and evil. So they called God a liar and went off on their own. Every one of us born into this world since then has had the same tendency. Every temptation offered us is offered wrapped up in a lie, like 'This is natural,' or 'This will make you happy,' or 'You deserve to get this.' God says, 'No temptation has seized you except what is common to man. And *God is faithful*; He will not let you be tempted beyond what you can bear. But when you are tempted, He will also provide a way out so that you can stand up under it' (1 Corinthians 10:13). To refuse a temptation, therefore, we have to identify truth in that area and choose truth through dependency on Christ.

"For example," I continued, "God made you to be a man. He also made women, and He engineered us to be attracted to the opposite sex. Every sin is a perversion of the truth, and that includes the one you are tempted with. But we can all be tempted into anything that is contrary to the clear testimony of God. Man functions that way all of his life. You've gone off in one way; other people go off in other ways. When we're choosing a lie, we are all saying the same thing as Adam: 'God, You don't know what You're talking about. This other thing is more fun than what You say.' It's usually afterward that we discover how tragic our choices can be. There is pleasure for a season, but there is also something inside of our own souls that starts eroding. We start paying a price of guilt, fear, depression, and self-hatred.

"But now, having been given new life in Christ, we can plug into Him to experience real meaning and purpose. We can walk daily in His unconditional love and acceptance. We can learn the fulfillment of being a servant to other people and seeing Christ use us in their lives.

"If you will step out in faith in Christ, Lee, presenting your daily experiences to Him for His evaluation of truth and error—and keep at it—you will find those desires dying down. Now, realize that there will always be the possibility of temptation. As long as you live in this body, you'll wrestle with the desires of the flesh, so you'll have to learn to make some wise choices to avoid unnecessary temptation. But over time, the Lord will renew your mind with His truth. That will, in turn, bring your emotions and desires more in line with who you really are—a new creature in Christ. Your daily decision, then, will be to apply Galatians 5:16: 'But I say, walk by the Spirit, and you will not carry out the desire of the flesh'" (NASB).

❦

I have seen Lee and many others like him go free from a terrible bondage through this message. The only solution is a total exchange. He first had to exchange an identity based on his behavior for an identity based on God's truth. Lee needed to recognize that at the moment he was born again, he had given Jesus all that he was and had received in return all that Christ is. As 1 Peter 2:24 says, "He Himself bore our sins in His body on the tree, so that we might die to sins and live for righteousness." Lee needed to learn not only to say "no" to sin, but to say "yes" to the Lord Jesus Christ who indwells him, to not only consider himself "dead to sin, but *alive to God* in Christ Jesus" (Romans 6:11).

Whatever you or I may be struggling with, the answer is the same. It is only through a total *exchange* that we will begin to see the *changes* we desire.

9

THE MINISTRY OF CONDEMNATION

L et's go now to Louisville, Kentucky," I said, as I punched one of the phone lines in our radio studio. "Marge, you're on *People to People.*"

"I just want to ask," said a quiet voice, "if it's possible for a Christian to commit suicide and still go to heaven."

It's a frightening thing to be put on a spot like that anywhere, much less on nationwide radio. Judging by her tone of voice, there was no mistaking her meaning. Marge wasn't asking out of mere curiosity. She was considering taking her own life. Christians are not immune to such thoughts and desires. In fact, their despair can in some ways be deeper because Christians are supposed to have found the answer to life's problems. When you have come to know God and still can't get your life straightened out, then where else can you go?

Can God fail? No, the answer to the problem is the same one we have already discussed from several angles: Truth sets you free; therefore, error is what binds you. My job with Marge was to discover and correct the errors in her mind that were causing such pain.

In this case, I was able to help Marge that evening to begin to experience the solution. But it also took time, good resources, Bible study, and personal help from one of our trained counselors in the Louisville area for Marge to really become free. But how can a Christian get so deep in the pits?

Marge had been a Christian for about six years. In the early days, she lived on a continual high of joy in the Lord. She immersed herself in the enthusiastic worship at her church, attended many seminars and, in her own words, was there "every time the doors were open." There was a great emphasis on "victory" at this church, with an attitude that Marge described as "you and Jesus can defeat anything."

"The only problem," she explained, "was that it wasn't working for me. I would go to the service and get all pumped up, but then get back in my problems the next day. So my life became like a roller coaster: all excited at church, but down in the dumps at home and at work.

"The speakers all taught that if there's some problem you can't beat, it's because you're not doing the right things. They all implied, 'If you're studying your Bible enough, if you're praying and fasting enough, if you're giving enough, then God will deliver you from your problems.' But I *was* giving, and I *was* studying, and I *was* praying and fasting and seeking God! But I still had financial problems. I was still a single mother raising a teenage son. I was still lonely. I was still struggling with being overweight. I was still angry. What was wrong? I was taught that if I did all the right things, then God would deliver me. But He didn't. The only thing I could assume was that God was rejecting me. He was refusing to help me for some reason.

"When I told the teachers about my struggles, they would always go back to me. They'd say that I must be allowing Satan to have a place in my heart. So back I'd go to confessing my anger and my overeating as sins, and to promise God to try harder to pray and fast and seek Him."

Marge's cyclical pattern of work, failure, and depression deepened to the point where, she said, "I was ready to put a gun to my head. I would get up and start driving to work, only to find myself weeping uncontrollably. I'd turn around and drive home, draw the curtains, and collapse on the couch for the day. Since I was afraid to kill myself, I prayed every night to God that I wouldn't wake up in the morning. Since He hated me so much, I couldn't see any reason why He wouldn't at least answer that prayer."

Law and Grace: The Issue of God's Acceptance

While Marge got to a level of depression and despair deeper than most people, the root of her bondage is actually a very common one. It is one I have experienced myself, and I find most Christians are tangled up in the same error to some extent. As a matter of fact, this error has plagued the Christian world for almost 2000 years. Indeed, it was the subject of the very first controversy encountered by the early church. The subject is law and grace.

I have found that few Christians are familiar with this topic. Those that have heard of law and grace tend to put it into the category of a stale theological subject. Nothing could be further from the truth! Law and grace is something that we are living every day, whether we know it or not. Law and grace involves how we are approaching our entire Christian lives, and the effects are far-reaching and profound. What you see in Marge's story is the result of a person living according to law. She is free today because she has learned what it means to live according to grace.

Let's clarify the issue. In the simplest of terms, this is what law and grace is all about: *Law and grace is the issue of God's acceptance.* In other words, on what basis is a man made acceptable to God? There are only three possible answers. Man is made (or tries to make himself) acceptable to God by law, by grace, or by a third, hybrid means called Galatianism. Let's look at each of them in turn.

1. Law

Under law, man is responsible to *make himself* acceptable to God by his work. You are accepted by God according to what you do or don't do. You can easily identify law by the presence of a small two-letter word: *if.* "*If* you do this, then God will accept you." Obviously, the opposite must also be true: "*If* you don't, He won't."

God's special relationship with the nation of Israel, called the Old Covenant or the law, began with this condition:

> Now *if you obey Me fully and keep My covenant,* then out of all nations you will be My treasured possession. Although the whole earth is Mine, you will be for Me a kingdom of priests and a holy nation (Exodus 19:5-6).

2. Grace

Under grace, God gives to man a standing of total acceptance as a *gift* through Jesus Christ. Man's work in no way contributes to God's acceptance of him. Once Jesus was asked, "'What must we do to do the works God requires?' Jesus answered, 'The work of God is this: to believe in the One He has sent'" (John 6:28-29). *By faith and faith alone a man receives the gift of righteousness in Christ*: "It is because of Him that you are in Christ Jesus, *who has become for us* wisdom from God—that is, *our righteousness, holiness* and *redemption*" (1 Corinthians 1:30).

Ephesians 2:8-9 is as direct a statement as you can find in the Bible: "For it is by grace you have been saved, through faith—and this not from yourselves, it is the gift of God—not by works, so that no one can boast."

3. Galatianism

The attempt to mingle law and grace, Galatianism takes many forms, but sooner or later it always ends up in a meaningless contradiction: "God's grace has made it possible for man to *work for* His acceptance and forgiveness," or "God loves us unconditionally *if* we keep all the rules." Law is the realm of what you *earn* by your performance. Grace is the realm of receiving a *free gift*. How could you ever mingle the two?

Imagine if a friend came up to you one day and said, "I'm going to give you a car! Absolutely free, for only $1000."

"Wait a minute," you say. "Did you say you're going to give me a car for free, or for $1000?"

"That's right," he says. "Absolutely free, for only $1000!"

That's gibberish! The word *free* by definition means with no payment due at all. You can't work for a gift, or it's not a gift. Even a payment of $1 takes it out of the realm of a gift. A gift is not a gift unless it is free.

> Other teachers would come through town to "help" the new believers and "correct" their understanding. "It's great that you believe in Jesus," they would say, "but that's not enough."

One day Tim Stevenson's seven-year-old daughter, Katie, was walking up and down their street with a wagon offering the other kids "free rides for a quarter."

"But Katie," said her mother, "you can't tell your friends it's free if you're going to charge them a quarter."

Katie replied, "But if I don't tell them it's free, nobody will want a ride!"

I have to laugh at Katie's salesmanship, but sadly it reminds me of how the gospel is often presented. People are attracted to Christ by the message of His total love and acceptance and of salvation by grace; then, once they're in the family of God, they are leveled by demands for performance and conformity. But the Bible says that we can't have it both ways. "And if by grace, then it is no longer by works; if it were, grace would no longer be grace" (Romans 11:6).

The problem is not new. The apostle Paul dealt with it throughout his entire ministry. Time and time again he would travel through a new region sharing the good news of Jesus Christ, leading thousands of people to salvation. Then after his departure other teachers would come through town to "help" the new believers and "correct" their understanding.

"It's great that you believe in Jesus," they would say, "but that's not enough. If you want to be acceptable to God, you've got to become circumcised according to the law of Moses. You've got to observe the Sabbath and other festivals. You've got to follow the dietary commands of the law." Along the way, these teachers—called Judaizers—would also attack Paul's credentials as a true apostle of Christ. This was the exact situation that prompted Paul's letter to the Galatians. His answer was as subtle as a meat cleaver:

> You foolish Galatians! Who has bewitched you? Before your very eyes Jesus Christ was clearly portrayed as crucified. I would like to learn just one thing from you: Did you receive the Spirit by observing the law, or by believing what you heard? Are you so foolish? After beginning with the Spirit, are you now trying to attain your goal by human effort? (Galatians 3:1-3).

The Galatian error has been the greatest thorn in the flesh of the church since the very beginning:

- In many places and times, it has been bold and straightforward. "You aren't saved by faith alone," it has been said, "but by faith plus good works." Actually, that error is pretty easy to deal with if you know the Bible.

- The version that is much more difficult and much more common is the one that drove Marge to despair. It is committed by groups that would swear up and down that a person is saved by God's grace through faith alone, that you can't do one thing to contribute to your salvation.

In this, they're right. The only problem is that their use of the word *salvation* is limited to your *initial* acceptance of Christ, the issue of where you go when you die. Here and now, though, they teach that God accepts you on the basis of your performance of certain rules and regulations. As a friend of mine says, when you're good you get the cookies; when you're bad you get the baseball bat. This return to the law is exactly what Paul is getting at in his question, "After beginning with the Spirit, are you now trying to attain your goal by human effort?" (Galatians 3:3).

Marge said to me, "It was made absolutely clear that you are saved only by faith in Jesus. But never was I taught that, as a Christian, faith is how you *live*. The emphasis was always on what I should be doing for God, and never on what God has already done and is committed to do for me."

What Marge described seems to be the experience of the majority of Christians today. As we saw in a previous chapter, love becomes practically meaningless apart from acceptance. Because of the mingling of law and grace, multitudes of Christians, who are absolutely certain that they are going to heaven when they die, are living in daily fear, frustration, and guilt. Believing that God is far away in disapproval, they are never free to discover Christ living in and through them.

Why the Law?

The reason that people persist in trying to bring law into the Christian life is that they have never come to grips with the real meaning and purpose of the law in the first place. While there were some general purposes of the law of Moses, such as to provide civil laws without which no society can function, its most important purposes relate to leading men to salvation.

First, *the law defines sin*. Romans 4:15 says that "where there is no law there is no transgression." In other words, you can't break a law that doesn't exist. Policemen couldn't pull you over and give you a ticket for speeding if the state did not have published and posted speed-limit laws. That's why Romans 5:13 says, "For before the law was given, sin was in the world. But sin is not taken into account when there is no law."

Second, *the law convicts men of their guilt and need for salvation*. The question is, Who will ever come to a Savior? The answer: only someone who knows he needs to be saved. The major purpose for which God gave the law was to convince men of their lost condition so that they would be prepared to accept Jesus Christ as Savior.

> Now we know that whatever the law says, it says to those who are under the law, *so that every mouth may be silenced and the whole world held accountable to God*. Therefore no one will be declared righteous in His sight by observing the law; rather, *through the law we become conscious of sin* (Romans 3:19-20).

What the Law Can't Do

It is very surprising to many people to discover that *the purpose of the law was never to make a man right with God*. All the law can do is to declare a standard and condemn a person for failure. It's just like a mirror. A mirror can show you that your face is dirty, but it cannot wash your face for you.

The law is like those pass/fail tests that I can remember having in school. Back then, I thought it was good news to have a pass/fail test—anything above a 70 was passing. But in regard to the law of God, the only acceptable grade is an unblemished 100 percent! It's pass/fail all right. You just have to be perfect, or you have failed and are doomed to judgment.

We love to compare ourselves to other people. There are others who are better, but you can always come up with somebody who is worse. But God is not comparing us to each other. If we are going to be measured according to our performance, there is only one standard—*perfection:* "For whoever keeps the whole law and yet stumbles at just *one point* is guilty of breaking *all* of it" (James 2:10). That, my friends, means in your entire lifetime!

The Very Bad News

In Galatians 3:10, Paul put it this way: "All who rely on observing the law are under a curse, for it is written, 'Cursed is everyone who does not continue to do *everything* written in the Book of the Law.'" The result of the law is a curse! Why? Because there is something wrong with the law? No. The problem is with us. The standard for acceptance under law is total perfection, "*everything* written in the Book of the Law." One failure brings you under the curse.

The amazing thing is that Paul is referring here just to the written law. Jesus Christ in His teaching ministry went beyond the written law to the real spirit and meaning behind it. He was talking to a generation who thought they were okay just because they were Jews. They thought they were righteous because they had not committed literal murder, for example. To shake up their cold complacency, Jesus magnified the inner heart of the law's demands:

> You have heard that it was said to the people long ago, "Do not murder, and anyone who murders will be subject to judgment." But I tell you that anyone who is angry with his brother will be subject to judgment (Matthew 5:21-22).

The Lord did the same thing with the law of adultery:

> You have heard that it was said, "Do not commit adultery." But I tell you that anyone who looks at a woman lustfully has already committed adultery with her in his heart (Matthew 5:27-28).

He went on to discuss many other issues, always going beyond the written law to the intent behind it. He summed up the law's demands in the statement, "Be perfect, therefore, as your heavenly Father is perfect" (Matthew 5:48). Christ is trying to hammer home the message that if you want to be accepted by God based on your own merits, the standard is perfection both inwardly and outwardly. It's no wonder that the crowds that heard Him were "amazed."

In 2 Corinthians 3:6, we are told that the law (here called "the letter") *kills*. In the same passage, the law is called "the ministry of *death*" (verse 7 NASB) and "the ministry of *condemnation*" (verse 9 NASB). "Why did

God give a law that would kill and condemn men?" many people ask me. I answer, "He did it to kill and condemn. When the law brings about death and condemnation, it is doing its job. That's what it is *supposed* to do." Because God is cruel? No! Because it is a necessary ministry to bring us to the salvation given through Jesus Christ! Galatians 3:23-24 puts it this way:

> Before this faith came, we were held prisoners by the law, locked up until faith should be revealed. *So the law was put in charge to lead us to Christ* that we might be justified by faith.

We look into the mirror of the law and see that we are lawbreakers and therefore under its curse. Desperately we cry out to God, "How can I be saved?" and the answer comes: "Believe in the name of the Lord Jesus Christ and you will be saved." Once we have come to this point, what further role does the law have in our lives? None! It has done its job! Its purpose was to drive us to Christ, and it has done so. "Now that faith has come, *we are no longer under the supervision of the law*" (Galatians 3:25).

The New Era

Many people ask, "But aren't we still supposed to keep the Ten Commandments?" Even ignoring the fact that nobody *could* keep them, there is another issue. I was asked this question by a pastor not long ago. I replied by asking him a question: "What did you do last Saturday?"

A little surprised, he answered, "I cut the grass and went fishing."

"Do you realize," I replied, "that if the Ten Commandments are still in effect, you should be taken out and stoned? The commandment is, 'Remember the Sabbath day by keeping it holy...On it you shall not do any work'" (Exodus 20:8,10).

He saw the point. Sunday is not the Sabbath. The actual Sabbath is from sundown Friday to sundown Saturday. The church has deliberately *not* worshipped on the Sabbath for 19 centuries. Today we have forgotten the reason for this tradition, but the early church knew. They were recognizing that God had done away with the old system, the law, and brought in something brand-new: a New Covenant, a new arrangement between God and man where time and place of worship no longer mattered. Every day is a day of Sabbath rest for those who are united with Christ Jesus.

The Old vs. the New

Recently at a seminar I was asked this question by a man named Mike: "But aren't nine of the Ten Commandments restated in the New Testament? And the New Testament is full of commands. What is the difference between those and being under the law?"

"That's a good question," I answered. "What we have to realize is that a law is not just a command. It is always a command *with a penalty attached*. For example, the speed law is not just 'You shall not drive over 55 miles per hour.' It is 'You shall not drive over 55, and if you do, you will pay a fine of up to $200.'

"You're right, Mike, that you see the same basic morality in the New Testament as in the Old. Right and wrong are still right and wrong because that is a reflection of God's character, and He doesn't change. But the difference is this: Under the law 'the wages of sin is death' (Romans 6:23); but 'There is now no condemnation for those who are in Christ Jesus' (Romans 8:1 NASB).

"That's one reason why the commands in the New Testament are not laws. The second reason is that we are not obeying those New Testament commands in order to be accepted by God. Under law, a man works in order to be accepted by God. Under grace, a man serves because he is *already* accepted by God!"

Man's difficulty in understanding the principles of law and grace is not a new phenomenon. Jesus encountered the same controversies. In fact, that is the background of the answer He gave to some critics who questioned Him on why He and His disciples did not observe all the legalistic traditions that had been passed down:

> Neither do men pour new wine into old wineskins. If they do, the skins will burst, the wine will run out and the wineskins will be ruined. No, they pour new wine into new wineskins, and both are preserved (Matthew 9:17).

In the winemaking process of that day, they would pour the new grape

juice into a wineskin. As the juice turned to wine through the fermentation process, it expanded and stretched the skins to their capacity. After
using that wine, they would never refill those skins with new wine. The
skins had already stretched as far as they could. If they had poured new
wine in them, the fermentation process would have begun and burst the
skins. The skins would have been ruined, and the wine lost as well.

> When you try to mingle the two…law is robbed of its terror
> and condemnation; grace is robbed of its freedom and joy.
> You end up with a gray no-man's-land.

Jesus is trying to tell them that the New Covenant that God is bringing into existence cannot be contained within the forms of the Old, the
law. Law and grace are opposing principles; they cannot be mixed. When
you try to mingle the two, you find that you have ruined both of them:
Law is robbed of its terror and condemnation; grace is robbed of its
freedom and joy. You end up with a gray no-man's-land where neither
can produce that for which it was created.

~≈~

Is it a serious matter to be under the law? Remember Marge. The
law kills. The law condemns. There is no hope under law. Again, not
because it is bad. When it does these things, it is doing exactly what
God intended it to do—so that our hearts would be prepared for His
solution: *"For Christ is the end of the law for righteousness to everyone who
believes"* (Romans 10:4 NASB).

"But this message will cause people to sin more," many people object.
Other people ask, "How does God lead us, if not by the law?" I'll discuss
the answers to those questions in the next chapters. Sufficient for now is
this announcement of our liberation: "For sin shall not be master over
you, for you are not under law but under grace" (Romans 6:14 NASB).

10

FREE FROM THE
YOKE OF SLAVERY

Wherever the pure message of God's love and acceptance in Jesus Christ has been shared, people have raised the same objection: "But you're giving people a license to sin." Actually, I have noticed that people are sinning quite well without a license, but that is beside the point. It's not a new issue; Paul faced it many times. In fact, he raised it himself in his letter to the Romans, knowing as he did what was going through people's minds as they listened to his explanation of the gospel: "What shall we say, then? Shall we go on sinning so that grace may increase?… What then? Shall we sin because we are not under law but under grace?" (Romans 6:1,15).

In both cases his answer is, "By no means!" It's as if he were saying, "What an absurd question!" And it *is* an absurd question when you understand the love and grace of God and know about Christ living in you. I have been asked it many times, and I like to answer with an illustration.

Imagine that you own a fine cafeteria. One day, you hear this tremendous commotion out in the alley where the garbage dumpsters are. You open the back door to see what's going on, and you see the most pitiful-looking human being you have ever seen in your life—me—fighting with several stray cats over the food scraps in the dumpster. I am a virtual living skeleton. It's obvious that I am living on the edge of starvation, and probably have been for a long time. There is nothing about me to provoke liking or affection in you, but you are moved to pity.

"Hey, hey!" you yell. "Get out of the garbage. Don't eat that stuff! Come over here." I trudge over to you, half-seeing you through hopeless eyes.

"Listen," you say. "I can't stand to see you eating garbage like that. Come into my cafeteria and eat."

"But I don't have any money," I reply.

"It doesn't matter," you say. "My chain of restaurants has done very well, and I can afford it. I want you to eat here every day from now on, absolutely free of charge!" You take my arm and lead me inside the restaurant. I cannot believe my eyes. I have never seen a cafeteria line before. With huge, unbelieving eyes I stare at the spread: vegetables...salads...fruits...beef...fish...chicken...cakes...pies...In my wildest dreams, I have never even imagined that such things could be.

I look at you intently. "Are you saying I can eat *anything* I want?"

"Yes, anything."

"Really, *anything* I want?" I ask again.

"Yes, I said anything you want," you answer.

Then slowly, with a gleam in my eye, I ask, "Can I eat some *garbage?*"

What would you think of me? You would think I was insane, wouldn't you? In the face of all that delicious food, all I can think of to ask is whether I can eat garbage. But that is exactly how I feel when people ask me if they can sin because they are under grace!

Getting Past the Sin Obsession

Jesus Christ laid down His life for us to take away, once and for all, our sins and guilt before a holy God. Then He gave *His life* to us to raise us from the dead spiritually. He gave us His righteousness, total acceptance, sonship in the family of God. He has made us to be

> a chosen people, a royal priesthood, a holy nation, a people belonging to God, that you may declare the praises of Him who called you out of darkness into His wonderful light (1 Peter 2:9).

The life that He has given us is *His* life: Jesus Christ living in and through us each and every day—an exciting adventure of being used by God to express His life and His love to people around us. And in the face of a "cafeteria line" like this, that Jesus called "abundant" life (John 10:10), all a person can think to ask is, "Does that mean that you can just go out and sin more?"

The Christian world is obsessed with sin. It's all we talk about. Most of our preaching and teaching is directed toward getting people to quit sinning. Are you ready for a really shocking statement? *The goal of the Christian life is not to stop sinning!* To use the analogy of the starving man, most Christian teaching is like a person following a starving man around saying, "You stay out of the garbage! Do you hear me? Don't eat the garbage! You stay out of there!" Look, when you're truly hungry, you'll eat anything—even garbage.

What should you do? I promise you: If you will get that man into the cafeteria line, and he begins experiencing what real, good food is like, he won't be nostalgically dreaming about the garbage out back.

What is it that every human being needs? The life of Christ! And not just our initial receiving of Him into our lives; we need to experience daily the reality of knowing Christ and walking with Him in a vibrant relationship. The Lord defined eternal life this way: "Now this is eternal life: that they may know You, the only true God, and Jesus Christ, whom You have sent" (John 17:3). *That is the real goal of the Christian life! Knowing Christ!*

It is only in comparison with the riches of knowing Christ that sin begins to lose its appeal. The longer that I am a Christian, the more I feel in my heart that sin is not just wrong, it is outright *stupid*. I feel so dumb for settling for anything less than experiencing Jesus Christ Himself every minute. Why should I ever wallow in the garbage when the Lord has laid a banquet table for me? And yet, the "stay-out-of-the-garbage" approach to Christian education predominates today.

Trying to Produce the Christian Life Through the Law

As we saw in the last chapter, when we try to use the law to generate the Christian life, we are missing the fact that the law was never given to make men right with God; it was given to show men their need so that they would turn to a Savior who would *make* them right with God. But there are other devastating results of using the law in the Christian life.

The Law Incites Us to Sin

First, we actually end up *producing* what we are trying to stop—*sin*. First Corinthians 15:56 says, "The sting of death is sin, and *the power of sin is the law.*" The law not only doesn't *stop* us from sinning, it actually stirs up *more*! Paul described his own experience this way:

> For I would not have known what it was to covet if the law had not said, "Do not covet." But sin, seizing the opportunity afforded by the commandment, *produced in me every kind of covetous desire.* For apart from the law, sin is dead (Romans 7:7-8).

Let's say you are walking down a sidewalk next to a wooden fence. In that fence is a hole. Most likely, it wouldn't attract your attention. You're thinking about other things. But now let's say that over the hole is a large white sign with these words written in big, red block letters: "Under no circumstances is anyone to look through this hole!" Now what happens to you? You know exactly what I mean. Suddenly there arises in you an irresistible drive—you *must* find out what's in there! All your ingenuity, creativity, and intelligence are bent on a single goal: "How can I get a look in there without getting caught?"

That is the universal experience of a sinful heart coming into contact with a law. The law stirs up rebellion in us. The problem is not the law. It is us. If you wave a red cape at a bull and it charges, you didn't create that nature in the animal. You just brought out its "bullishness." In the same way, the more that you try to use the law to make people live the Christian life, the more you stir up sinful, rebellious desires in them.

The Law Deals Only with the Outside

The second reason that the law is useless for producing the life that God desires is that it deals only with *externals*. God, we are told, is looking on man's heart, but the law only deals with his actions. If merely shaping up our actions were what God desired, then the Pharisees would have been His favorites. But Jesus reserved His harshest statements for them, who seemed to be the ultimate in outward righteousness:

> Woe to you, teachers of the law and Pharisees, you hypocrites! You clean the outside of the cup and dish, but inside they are full of greed and self-indulgence...You are like whitewashed tombs,

which look beautiful on the outside but on the inside are full of dead men's bones and everything unclean. In the same way, on the outside you appear to people as righteous but on the inside you are full of hypocrisy and wickedness (Matthew 23:25,27-28).

And that is the *best* that the law can produce!

These same self-righteous Pharisees were willing to condemn and crucify the Lord Jesus Christ on trumped-up charges. *At the very same instant,* they refused to enter Pontius Pilate's home for fear of being "defiled" and made unfit to observe the Passover! The spirit of Pharisaism is still with us today. It's the attitude that being a good Christian means "I don't drink, smoke, or chew, or run around with the girls who do."

The Bible tells us that "without faith it is impossible to please God" (Hebrews 11:6). As a matter of fact, it goes so far as to say that "everything that does not come from faith is *sin*" (Romans 14:23). Yet the Bible makes this clear distinction: "*The law is not based on faith*; on the contrary, 'The man who *does* these things will live by them'" (Galatians 3:12). A life of faith and a life based on the law are continually presented as being exact opposites in the Scriptures.

> If you buy into this mind-set, you can never rest. Man's ingenuity at coming up with new and more complicated laws is amazing.

Do we live by faith? What's that? Do we love anybody? Who cares? Just make sure you're toeing the line. As a result, Christians get better known for what they are *against* than for what they are *for*. The meanest, most unloving people on earth are legalists. And like the Pharisees, they are capable of feeling extremely righteous even in the act of stabbing a brother in the back.

We do all the right things (by our own definition) and don't do the wrong things, so we feel we are good Christians. But if you buy into this mind-set, you can never rest. Man's ingenuity at coming up with new and more complicated laws is amazing. From the hundreds of examples I could give you, here are just four:

Example #1. Mark called *People to People* to ask what it means to be free in God's grace. "I've been taught practically nothing but legalism," he said. One of his examples was this: "I've been told that on Sundays it's okay to shoot a few baskets, but I shouldn't play a game of basketball."

"Mark," I answered, "the Bible teaches that the law stirs up sin, and I'll tell you what's going through my mind. I'm wondering if that applies to a half-court game, or just full-court basketball. How about one-on-one? Or what about a game of H-O-R-S-E? I hear a law, and immediately start looking for loopholes!

"Do you see what I mean?" I continued. "It's just like the Pharisees in the time of Jesus. They had the laws of God, but that wasn't good enough. So they invented a few hundred of their own. In that time, for example, it was okay on the Sabbath to spit on a rock, but you couldn't spit on the dirt because that would make clay, making clay was work, and you couldn't work on the Sabbath."

Example #2. There is a fascinating story in John chapter 9 where Jesus healed a blind man by spitting on the ground, rubbing the mud on the man's eyes, and instructing him to wash in a certain pool. The Lord certainly didn't need the mud—He healed many other people with just a touch or a word—so I often wondered why He did this. Then I discovered the Pharisees' interpretation of spitting on the ground as violating the Sabbath, and that provided the answer. The blind man was healed on the Sabbath. In my opinion, Jesus went through this procedure *specifically because* it violated the Pharisees' law! It was a deliberate dig at the foolishness of their legalism.

The hypocrisy of these legalists is clearly revealed in their reaction to the man's healing. Do they rejoice with the man because he can see for the first time? No. Do they give praise to God for the miracle? No. Do they consider the claims of Christ since He has demonstrated His authority? No. They couldn't care less about these things. "We know this man [Jesus] is a sinner" (John 9:24). How do they know this? Because according to their traditions He violated the Sabbath. "Don't confuse us with facts or miracles," they say. "Our minds are made up."

Isn't that ridiculous? But that's exactly what happens under the law. You immediately start looking for loopholes, wondering about exceptions, and you start having to make them more and more complicated to cover all the possible situations. Then, once you've erected this elaborate system, .

you are obligated to defend it against any challenge. As much as any other factor, *job security* was the motivation of those who killed Jesus.

Example #3. I once counseled a young woman named Lisa, who had a unique problem. She told me that she was unable to go shopping. I asked her why. "I was raised in a very strict group where we were never allowed to listen to secular music," she said. "In fact, they said that the devil inspired all music that is not about Jesus. They told us that we would go to hell if we listened very long to any music on the radio or records, so I never did.

"But the problem is," she continued, "that almost all stores play music over the loudspeakers. I went into a clothing store the other day and they were playing a country music radio station. I broke out in a sweat and felt so guilty that I had to leave—even though I know now that God is not that way."

Even though Lisa, a 28-year-old woman, had come to truly know Jesus Christ in a personal way, she still found it extremely hard to shake off that early conditioning. Can you imagine? Not even able to go shopping because of intense guilt feelings? Now that's bondage!

Example #4. I'll never forget going on a couples' retreat at a camp one time. There were about eight married couples, all good friends, enjoying the pool area together, when this man came running up, looking like he was having a fit.

"Everybody out of the pool!" he yelled. We asked him what was the matter.

"There's no mixed swimming allowed at this camp," he said.

I walked up to him and asked, "What do you mean: 'no mixed swimming'?"

"Men and women aren't allowed to use the pool at the same time," he explained. I pointed out to him that we were all married couples, but he said it didn't matter.

"Are you trying to tell me," I asked, "that I can sleep with my wife at this camp, but I can't *swim* with her?"

"Right," he said.

Almost always, there are explanations given for such rules and regulations that sound very logical and reasonable. But the apostle Paul warned sternly against submitting to them, and added this assessment:

Such regulations indeed have an *appearance* of wisdom, with their self-imposed worship, their false humility and their harsh treatment of the body, *but they lack any value in restraining sensual indulgence* (Colossians 2:23).

A hundred years ago, women wore long dresses revealing only their faces and hands. Today, in strict Muslim areas, they go even further. They cover a woman entirely. Now I ask you: Do you believe that lust is eliminated under those conditions? No, in fact lust is actually increased. Man's imagination is always more titillating than what his eyes actually see. We simply refuse to face the fact that our sin problem arises from our own hearts! And *the law can do nothing to change a heart.*

The Law Involves Human Effort

The third reason that the law cannot produce the life that God desires is that *law is the realm of self-effort.* This is the real lesson of a famous passage of Scripture:

> I do not understand what I do. For what I want to do I do not do, but what I hate I do…So I find this law at work: When I want to do good, evil is right there with me. For in my inner being I delight in God's law; but I see another law at work in the members of my body, waging war against the law of my mind and making me a prisoner of the law of sin at work within my members (Romans 7:15,21-23).

People have argued for centuries over whether this passage describes Paul's experience as a lost man or as a Christian. I have an opinion myself, but that's beside the point. In the controversy, we have failed to see that the real issue here is that *Paul is describing the experience of a man who is trying to live according to the law!* The experience he describes is the result *regardless* of whether you are a lost man or a Christian.

This is the predictable, universal experience of any person who sincerely tries to live up to God's standards on his own. Whether before *or after* we become Christians, we have no ability in and of ourselves to keep the law. Moreover, it is always those persons who care the most, who are the most sincere, that the law wrecks. Someone who is complacent and apathetic can sit and listen to legalism for years without much damage; it just goes in one ear and out the other. But someone who deeply desires to seek God and to please Him, and who tries to live the Christian life on his own, will crash and burn like Marge, whose story I told in the last chapter.

The law will always drive you eventually to Paul's conclusion in Romans 7:24: "What a wretched man I am! Who will rescue me from this body of death?" And the law will drop you right there.

The Law Can Only Expose the Problem

Remember, the law shows man his need, but not the solution. Its purpose was to bring people the knowledge of their sin and guilt so that they would turn to Jesus Christ as Savior. Immediately after saying, "Who will rescue me...?" Paul rejoices with "Thanks be to God—through Jesus Christ our Lord!" (Romans 7:25).

Now that the law has done its job in showing us our utter inability to live up to God's righteousness on our own and we have turned to Jesus Christ in total dependency, God does not want us to return to the law. "Now that faith has come, we are no longer under the supervision of the law" (Galatians 3:25).

If we still think that we can earn God's acceptance or live the Christian life on our own, it is a sign that the law has not really completed its work in our lives. Every Christian knows that he has committed *sins*, but it's another thing to realize that we are "wretched men." The first is an admission that we have done some wrong *actions;* the second is a realization that the problem is deeper than just what we have done wrong; it is *ourselves.*

Salvation is not just a release from punishment that we deserve. It is truly being rescued from what we *are.* It's like the famous line from the cartoon strip *Pogo:* "We have met the enemy, and he is *us*." The issue of law and grace boils down to a simple decision: Will we embrace God's definition of the true objectives of the Christian life, or will we pursue our own man-made definitions of success in the Christian life? Is it our objective to please God, or men?

A Legalist's Work Is Never Done

I realize that I haven't yet addressed the question, "If we are not to live under the law, how *do* we live?" The next chapter will address that issue directly. But until we see that the law can never accomplish God's desire in our lives, we will not be willing to put it aside to receive His true way of life.

When Christians are living under law, the results are the same as they have always been. And it doesn't matter whether you are trying to live up to God's laws, man-made laws, or even your own self-imposed standards. The result will be fear, guilt, frustration, and feelings of condemnation. You will experience a lack of ability to love God or men. How can you love a God that you are laboring to please but never can? And when you are feeling continual guilt and condemnation, how can you be kind and forgiving to other people? When they appear to be doing well, you envy them. When they fail, you judge them. After all, why should I let *you* off the hook if God is hammering *me* every time I blow it? That's the way you think under law.

Under law you never experience peace or rest in the Christian life. Why? Because your work is never done. A "spiritual restlessness" results, where you are always looking for the "something more" that will transform your Christian life into reality. It's always around the corner: at the next seminar, on the next Web site, in finding that spiritual experience— never resting in Christ Himself, who lives in you, who has already done it all, who has already given you everything you need.

Hypocrites and Rebels

Under law we become hypocrites. The word comes from the Greek theater. A hypocrite is not an imperfect person; a hypocrite is an *actor*, a *pretender*. What made the Pharisees hypocrites was not their faults; it was their pretense that they were righteous. It was teaching one thing and doing another. But that is what law will always produce: people who are always hiding their real selves, always acting, always pretending, never being real.

But what happens when we are set free by grace? One of the most common testimonies I hear is, "For the first time in my life, I am free to just be myself! I'm free to be me."

The ultimate consequence of living under law is outright rebellion— when you give up because of the hopelessness of ever making it. I can't tell you the number of times I have sat in a counseling office with someone who has said, "I've been rebelling against God for ten years. I walked away from Christianity, and I'm mad at God."

"Tell me about the God you've been angry at and rebelling against," I ask them.

> I have never heard anyone say, "I've had it! I quit! I'm sick to death of the love and grace of God. I'm sick of other Christians loving and accepting me."

When they describe what they have been rebelling against, I have often replied, "Good! You *should* have been rebelling against that god and against that religion! Now let me tell you about the *real* God and His real Son, Jesus Christ. About the God who loves you and accepts you unconditionally."

Time and time again, I have seen these people who have been branded as "rebels against God" or "backslidden Christians" come out of their chairs in excitement and joy as they learn for the first time about the incredible grace, love, and acceptance of God in Jesus Christ.

In all my years as a Christian, I have never heard anyone say, "I've had it! I quit! I'm sick to death of the love and grace of God. I'm sick of other Christians loving and accepting me. I'm giving up this Christian life." No, I've never heard that. But I couldn't count the number of Christians I've known who have given up because of being under law, who have been broken by the crushing burden of trying to be good enough to earn God's acceptance, who have been mangled by the competition, the judging, and the demands to conform to some group's standards. "We'll accept you if you look like, walk like, talk like, and act like *us*." And the implication is always, "And God will, too."

Standing Firm in Grace

So what *are* we to do?

First, we must apply Paul's exhortation in Galatians 5:1: "It is for freedom that Christ has set us free. Stand firm, then, and do not let yourselves be burdened again by a yoke of slavery." What is the "yoke of slavery"? The law! We have been set free, Paul proclaims. Don't let yourselves be put back under the law. Peter echoed these words in his answer to the Judaizers: "Now then, why do you try to test God by putting on the necks of the disciples a yoke that neither we nor our fathers have been able to bear?" (Acts 15:10).

Jesus Christ came to free us from the burden of the law by calling us to a life united with His:

> Come to Me, all you who are weary and burdened, and I will give you *rest*. Take *My yoke* upon you and learn from Me, for I am gentle and humble in heart, and you will find rest for your souls. For *My yoke is easy and My burden is light* (Matthew 11:28-30).

Paul doesn't stop with his exhortation to stand firm in our freedom, though. He also issues a warning: "Mark my words! I, Paul, tell you that if you let yourselves be circumcised, Christ will be of no value to you at all" (Galatians 5:2).

This is an amazing statement. Paul earlier in the letter recognized that they were truly born again. Under what possible circumstances could you ever say to a Christian that Christ would be of no benefit to him? The answer comes in verse 3: "Again I declare to every man who lets himself be circumcised that *he is obligated to obey the whole law.*"

Law and Grace Cannot Coexist

You will find that a characteristic of legalists is that they always want to "cherry-pick" their favorite laws. Nobody ever tries to keep them all; they just want to hold on to their favorites. But Paul is stressing the fact that you are either under law or under grace. You can't be under grace and continue to hold on to even *one law*. Reliance on just one law to make you acceptable to God brings you into the *entire realm* of law. That's why Paul says later in the chapter, "A little yeast works through the whole batch of dough" (Galatians 5:9).

It takes only one law to spoil the entirety of grace. You can't be trusting what *you* do and what Jesus Christ has done at the same time! Paul finishes his argument with a shocking statement: "You who are trying to be justified by law have...fallen away from grace" (Galatians 5:4). This verse has been taken out of context countless times to threaten

Christians that they will lose their salvation if they commit too many sins. That is a tremendous error:

- First, the phrase "fallen away from grace" has nothing to do with losing your salvation. You can clearly see from the context that it means to fall out of the freedom of grace back into the slavery of the law!

- Second, it's not those Christians who have committed certain sins that have "fallen away from grace." It says, "You who are trying to be justified by law" are the ones who have fallen from grace. In other words, the very people who would maintain that you can either gain God's acceptance by your performance or lose it by your failures are the ones this verse is talking about. *Legalists* are the ones who have fallen from grace!

We are beloved, accepted children of God, who have been called to His "banquet table" to experience Jesus Christ living in and through us every day. Abundant life is not "pie-in-the-sky" or nebulous theory. It is real, and it is ours for the taking if we will only believe. Let's not settle for anything less.

11

LIVING BY A HIGHER LAW

At a seminar, a young man named David raised a question. "Bob, maybe I'm dense, but I can't quite get a handle on what you mean by 'legalism.' I can see it clearly if someone is adding conditions to being saved, but how do you spot legalism in the everyday Christian life?" He went on to elaborate. "I can see how people can be under the law and doing Bible study, witnessing, giving money, and so on. But the problem is this: Certainly *God* wants us to do those things! And He doesn't want us to steal, or lie, or punch anybody out. What makes something legalistic or not legalistic?"

Where Does Your Motive Originate?

David asked an excellent question! We often throw around terms like *legalism* without defining them. Here's how I answered him. "There are two major areas which determine if something is legalistic or not," I said. "First of all, the *motive* for the action. In other words, *why* are you doing or not doing something? Remember law and grace and the issue of God's acceptance.

"Let's take witnessing, for example. Why are you doing it? One person is witnessing in an attempt to gain God's acceptance. He doesn't want to do it, but he does because he thinks he has to. Another man is sharing Christ, too. But the second man knows that he is already accepted by God because of Jesus Christ, and he is witnessing out of genuine concern and love for people. So you have two people doing outwardly the same activity: The first man is living under law; the second is living under grace. The motive makes the difference.

"It is said that confession is good for the soul but hard on the reputation, but I have to admit that I know from experience what it means to share Christ in the power of the flesh (legalistically). I can't tell you the number of times I talked to a man about the Lord, the whole time looking out of the corner of my eye to see if anyone was watching me and noticing how 'spiritual' I was. Although God used His Word in those situations to lead many people to Himself, my attitude was certainly not what He was looking for."

Where Is the Source of Your Life?

"Do you see what I mean, David?" I asked. He nodded, so I continued. "The second factor that makes something legalistic or not is the *source of the life*. Law is the realm of self-effort. A life under grace is exemplified by the resurrected Christ living in and through you."

There's an illustration I shared with David that day that, I find, clearly explains the difference between legalism and real Christianity. Imagine yourself in a large house, in which are living both deaf and hearing people. They are all mixed together, and you can't tell by looking who is deaf and who has hearing. Sitting in a room by himself is a man. As you watch, you notice that he is tapping his toes rhythmically and snapping his fingers in time. You know what is happening. He's listening to music, and obviously enjoying himself. His whole body wants to respond to what his ears are receiving. There's nothing strange or mysterious about it.

But now, let's add a new person to the scene. One of the deaf persons opens the door and enters the room. He immediately sees the first man and walks over to him and smiles a greeting. The deaf man watches the music-lover for a few moments. "He sure seems to be enjoying himself," he thinks. "I think I'll try it, too." So the deaf man sits next to the first man and begins to imitate him. Awkwardly and haltingly at first, he tries to snap his fingers, tap his toes, and move like the person next to him. Everybody has some sense of rhythm, whether they can hear or not. After a little practice, the deaf man is snapping and tapping in time with the first man. He even smiles a little and shrugs: "It's not *that* much fun," he thinks, "but it's okay."

Let's now add our final factor to the story. A third man walks into the room. What does he see? *Two men, apparently doing the same thing.* But is there a difference? Absolutely! All the difference in the world! The first man's actions are natural *responses* to the music he hears. The deaf man is only *imitating* those outward actions—even though he can't hear a note. *That* is the difference between real Christianity and legalism!

When we are approaching the Christian life in the way God intended, our attitudes and actions are a response to the "music" we hear. That music is our personal relationship with the living Christ who indwells us. It's the music of walking in a trust relationship with a loving God and Father that we are learning to love more and more every day.

> The grace and love of God are the true motivation for the Christian life...That's the real music which should be the source of our lives.

On the other hand, a legalist couldn't care less if you are stone-deaf to the love and grace of God. All legalism cares about is getting people to tap and snap at the right time! The legalist will always say that an emphasis on grace will lead to more sinning. But that's not what the Bible says!

> For the grace of God that brings salvation has appeared to all men. It [the "grace of God"!] teaches us to say "No" to ungodliness and worldly passions, and to live self-controlled, upright and godly lives in this present age, while we wait for the blessed hope—the glorious appearing of our great God and Savior, Jesus Christ (Titus 2:11-13).

The grace and love of God are the true motivation for the Christian life—not according to me, according to the Bible. That's the real music which should be the source of our lives.

What's the Goal of Living by the Spirit?

The most important biblical terms which refer to this principle are "walk by the Spirit" (Galatians 5:16 NASB) and "be filled with the Spirit" (Ephesians 5:18). But it is right here that many Christians become very frustrated. I have heard them exclaim, "I've heard those phrases all my life, but I don't have any idea what they're talking about. Everybody says to do it, but nobody tells me *how* to do it!" I can honestly say that I can understand their frustration, because I've been there myself.

Soon after I received Christ, I was taught that daily Christian living was through "appropriating the power of the Holy Spirit." That sounded good, but I asked how you do it. The answer was, "You are filled with the Spirit by faith." That sounded good, too. After all, everybody knows how important faith is. So I tried it.

I would be sitting in my office, then realize that I hadn't asked to be filled with the Spirit that day. So I would confess all the sins I could remember, then claim God's promise that He would do anything I asked according to His will (1 John 5:14-15). Since it was obviously His will that I be filled with the Spirit, I would ask for the experience "by faith." According to what I had been taught, I was now filled with the Spirit, my assurance based on the fact that I had claimed God's promise and was believing Him for the answer. But I was still sitting in my office chair, and I didn't feel a bit different.

My experience just didn't seem to match up with the quality of *life* that is described throughout the New Testament, particularly in the book of Acts, where several times the apostles and other believers are described as being filled with the Spirit. On the other hand, there was certainly a lot of witnessing going on in the book of Acts. Since I was an enthusiastic and faithful witness—more due to my salesman's personality than to the work of the Spirit—I assumed that I must be filled with the Spirit, too. I therefore pushed aside my doubts.

The Missing Central Element

What brought this issue to a head in my life was the task of writing Bible study booklets. I had written two series—one on the deity of Christ and another on the authority of the Word of God—and I was beginning a third on daily Christian living. Subjects planned were Christ's finished work on the cross, the ministry of the Holy Spirit, the conflict between the Spirit and the flesh, and so on. The final lesson was to be "How to

Love." I expected to breeze right through this series; after all, I was just writing out what I had been teaching in seminars for many years. And it was a breeze—until I came to that last lesson on love.

Trying to write that last lesson became one of the most frustrating, nerve-racking experiences of my life! Naturally, to write a Bible study lesson you have to define terms and have a plan of action to help the student understand the subject. But I couldn't do it. My outlines and explanations just seemed to wander around in circles and never get anywhere. There were even a few occasions where our staff met together to discuss the lesson on love, and we got into heated arguments about what love *is*! I was ready to tear my hair out.

Finally, it seemed that God got into my brain the message He had been trying to send: "Bob, did it ever occur to you that the reason you're not able to write a lesson on love is *because you don't know anything about love?*" That brought me up short. As I mulled over that thought, it became obvious to me that God was right. I really *didn't* know anything about love, or at least not nearly as much as I thought I did. God seemed to be saying, "Let's go back to square one and start all over."

I went back to lesson one—"Christ's Finished Work on the Cross"— and, in the course of the massive research and study that was necessary, God began to teach me out of His Word how great is His total forgiveness in Christ Jesus. I began to learn as never before how complete was His work for our reconciliation and forgiveness. I began to see His unconditional love and acceptance to a depth that I never dreamed possible as I was understanding the finality of the cross for the first time. I started to get so excited and full of joy that I kept our whole office in an uproar for weeks by my wandering from room to room, starting conversations about what God was teaching me.

Empowered to Love

Normally, I find, God allows me to see a truth in His Word, and then He shows me in a real-life situation what it *means*. It was at this time that I had one of the most vivid learning experiences of my life, an incident that showed me how God's love and forgiveness practically work themselves out in our lives.

As I was preparing to go to work one morning, I gave my teenage daughter, Debbie, the assignment of picking up peaches which had dropped from a tree in our backyard. When I came home that evening and discovered that she hadn't done it, I went into her room to discover why not. Debbie's only response was, "There were bees out there."

To this day I don't know why, but that answer seemed totally unreasonable to me and I went into a rage. I totally lost my temper and blasted Debbie with everything I had. I ranted, and raved, and yelled, and made a total fool out of myself.

A few minutes later, I was in my own bedroom, feeling guilty and embarrassed. What do you do in that situation? Well, I got down on my knees at the bed to do what I had always done, and what I had been taught to do: I started to ask God for His forgiveness. "O Lord, I have been really stupid. *Please* forgive me."

For some reason, although this was a scene I had experienced many times before, my prayer rang totally hollow that day. In my heart, it was as if God were saying, "Bob, I have already forgiven you. What do you think happened at that cross 2000 years ago?" In light of all I had been learning about the finality of the cross, I realized that I was asking God to do something that He had already done once and for all.

I took a different angle in my prayer. "But Lord, I am so sorry for losing my temper."

"Are you really sorry, Bob?"

"Ooòh, Lord, I am *sorry!*"

"Then go tell Debbie."

I nearly choked. "I'm not *that* sorry, Lord."

The struggle went on in my heart for the longest time, but I finally caught loud and clear what God had been teaching me for many months. "Don't you see, Bob, that the problem is not between you and Me? You have insulted My daughter, Debbie, and she's in her room crying. The problem is between you and her. If you love Me, then go be reconciled to *her.*"

That day I discovered what the power of the Holy Spirit is. It took no power at all for me to ask God for His forgiveness—that was easy. But it took the power of the Holy Spirit, several angels, and a few mules thrown in to get me to go to my daughter, *whom I had really hurt,* to tell *her* I was wrong and to ask her for *her* forgiveness! After my internal struggle, I went back to Debbie's room and said, "Debbie, I'm sorry. I acted like a man who doesn't even know the Lord. Please forgive me, and let me share what God has taught me through this experience." Soon we were both crying and hugging one another. The problem was not only solved, but God brought us even closer together than before.

Truly Seeing God's Love

Now, all this was occurring just a few months after my desperate prayer offered while driving down the freeway to work. I had prayed, "Lord, take me back to the days when I first knew You." Now He was doing that and more. And the key that unlocked the door was *seeing God's love for me*. "But God demonstrates His own love toward us, in that while we were yet sinners, Christ died for us" (Romans 5:8 NASB).

As I looked back over my Christian life, this illustration seemed to describe me: In those early days, I was like a brand-new twig on the grapevine. I wasn't very big or very mature, and I couldn't support much fruit, but I was totally full of the life of the vine—the love of Christ. Then I began to grow. But that growth was characterized by things like knowledge, experience, and more conformity to the Christians around me. I was bigger and apparently more mature, but the fruit wasn't there. I became filled with knowledge instead of Christ.

Before, in evangelistic opportunities, I may have been awkward, but I was overflowing with the love of Jesus and sharing out of genuine concern. But then I started sharing my knowledge, full of nifty illustrations and snappy comebacks, and I wondered where the power went. Why didn't I see the same results as before, when I had become so much more sophisticated in my presentation?

Once again it seemed as if God was sending me a message: "You used to share *Me* with people, Bob. Now you share your knowledge." As I was becoming preoccupied with what I was learning about God's love and grace, though, I found myself excitedly sharing Christ again. And I started seeing the results again.

I found my reactions to other people changing, too. I had always been a hard-driving, demanding businessman, and I had brought those qualities into my Christian life. But now I discovered affection, genuine concern, forgiveness, and even tenderness coming out of me toward my family and staff. In other words, I found myself experiencing Christ's love toward other people. The kind of love that is described in 1 Corinthians 13:

> Love is patient, love is kind. It does not envy, it does not boast, it is not proud. It is not rude, it is not self-seeking, it is not easily angered, it keeps no record of wrongs. Love does not delight in evil but rejoices with the truth. It always protects, always trusts, always hopes, always perseveres. Love never fails (1 Corinthians 13:4-8).

This kind of love is not a feeling—it's an attitude that is exemplified by certain actions. But while for years I had recognized 1 Corinthians 13 love as the measure, I never got much closer to being able to do it. But now I found that love was becoming real in me—without a struggle or even conscious effort. How did it happen?

How God Loves Us

The insight that God gave me in answer to this question was like a switch that lights up an entire house. I saw that 1 Corinthians 13 doesn't just describe the love that we ought to have for one another; I saw that *this is a description of how God loves us!*

Imagine the implications! How does God love you? Substitute "God is" for "love is" in the passage, and see what it does for your own heart.

> God is always patient with you. God is always kind to you. God does not envy, He does not boast, He is not proud. God is not rude to you, He is not self-seeking, He is never easily angered with you. God keeps no record of your wrongs. God does not delight in evil but rejoices with the truth. He always protects you, always trusts you, always hopes the best for you, always perseveres with you. God's love for you never fails.

Is this a valid application? Absolutely! The Bible says, *"God is love"* (1 John 4:8). I have shared this with many individuals in counseling situations and seen their eyes get large with wonder. "Do you mean that *that's* the way God loves me?" they say. It seems too good to be true.

As I was learning about God's love, it made several other scriptural passages come alive:

> A new command I give you: Love one another. *As I have loved you*, so you must love one another (John 13:34).

> Accept one another, then, *just as Christ accepted you*, in order to bring praise to God (Romans 15:7).

> Be kind and compassionate to one another, forgiving each other, *just as in Christ God forgave you* (Ephesians 4.32).

Do you see the common theme? How are we in the body of Christ to love, accept, and forgive one another? Just as God in Christ has loved, accepted, and forgiven us! Seeing this, I recognized that this is a law of human nature. Whether we realize it or not, *we will treat other people with the same measure of love, acceptance, and forgiveness that we (rightly or wrongly) think we are receiving from God.* We will never love one another with a higher degree of love than we think we are receiving from God. In other words, if I think that God likes me when I'm good but is hammering me when I'm bad, how do you think I'll treat you? Exactly the same way!

> Our concept of God's love and grace is an issue that affects every area of our lives, especially our relationships... I have seen all kinds of personal and family problems traced back to a faulty understanding of God's love.

I don't think I've ever met a Christian who, sometime in his life, didn't ask the question, "Why don't we find more love in the church?" To me it has become a simple answer. "The reason that there's not more love in the church is because of a lack of understanding of *God's love* in the church." Religious people can become so mean because (in their own minds) they're serving a mean God. That's why aggressively defending the message of God's grace against legalism is not just nitpicking the Scriptures. Our concept of God's love and grace is an issue that affects every area of our lives, especially our *relationships*. In my counseling office,

I have seen all kinds of personal and family problems traced back to a faulty understanding of God's love.

The Spirit's Power Enables Us to Comprehend God's Love

Through these insights, and especially in Ephesians 3:14-21, I finally found the solution to my quest for understanding what it means to be filled with the Spirit. In this passage, Paul prays for the Ephesians that God would "strengthen you with power through His Spirit in your inner being" (verse 16). The prayer for "power" caught my attention, because what he goes on to say was so different from what I expected. I had always prayed for power to *do* things. But Paul implied that we need power for something else:

> And I pray that you, being rooted and established in love, may have power...*to grasp how wide and long and high and deep is the love of Christ, and to know this love that surpasses knowledge—* that you may be filled to the measure of all the fullness of God (Ephesians 3:17-19).

What do we need power for? To understand the love of Christ! And what is the result of knowing the love of Christ that "surpasses knowledge"? We will be *filled to the measure of all the fullness of God*"! There, finally, was the answer I was looking for, a practical explanation of what it means to be filled with the Spirit: *To be filled with the Spirit is to be totally filled with the knowledge of God's love and grace in Jesus Christ.*

How practical it is! Taken out of context, the command in Ephesians 5:18 to "be filled with the Spirit" sounds mystical and even magical. But two chapters earlier, Paul told us what it means. In 5:18 the comparison to being drunk with wine, as has been pointed out by many other people, shows that being "filled" means to be totally under the influence of something to the point of being controlled by it. If you are filled with wine, what controls you? Wine. If you are filled with anger, what controls you? Anger. If you are totally filled with the knowledge of God's love and grace, what controls you? The love of God! And when you are full of God's love, there's nothing that will stop it from spilling over onto other people.

Living in Love

The love of God in our hearts produces a response that is as irresistible as music to our bodies. Presenting our minds and bodies to an indwelling Lord who loves us perfectly becomes a joy. The Christian life doesn't feel unnatural when your mind is full of God's grace; it feels truly natural for the first time.

This isn't to imply that there's no struggle or no need to exercise our wills. The flesh continues to set "its desire against the Spirit, and the Spirit against the flesh; for these are in opposition to one another, so that you may not do the things that you please" (Galatians 5:17 NASB). The flesh continues to send messages to our minds, appealing to fear, anger, lust, and selfishness. But we don't have to live in bondage to those things. God's answer is also given: "But I say, walk by the Spirit, and you will not carry out the desire of the flesh" (Galatians 5:16 NASB).

This verse is as important for what it does *not* say as for what it *does* say. Notice that it didn't say that the desires of the flesh will go away. As long as we live in fallen bodies, we will feel that influence. It also didn't say, "Clean up the flesh, and then you'll be spiritual." It seems to me that vast amounts of Christian teaching is saying this very thing. It can never work.

- Number one, you can work throughout your life and never get the flesh cleaned up. Christ didn't come to improve the flesh; He came to execute it and to give us new life. Trying to clean ourselves up is merely returning to the law—the ultimate exercise in futility.

- Number two (using the illustration at the start of the chapter), this error of cleaning ourselves up is like saying, "If you'll tap and snap correctly, you'll hear the music." No. God wants us to listen to His music—the message of His unconditional love and acceptance—and *then* respond to what we hear!

God's love working in our hearts deals with us on a level of sensitivity that neither the law nor self-discipline can ever reach. An illustration that taught me this personally was an incident with my son, Bob, when he was about ten years old.

I was reading the Bible one day at my office, really enjoying a time with God. In the course of praying about things on my mind, I asked, "Lord, I want to be the kind of person You want me to be. If there's an area that's wrong that I'm not aware of, show it to me." I was totally surprised by what came to my mind.

Each Sunday after church, we had a family habit of going out to lunch. Each week, it started out as a fun family time. But it seemed that we always ended up with tension in the air. I began to wonder why. As I thought about those lunches, I imagined a scene that had occurred many times. Bobby was an enthusiastic, growing young boy, and he really liked going out to restaurants. He especially liked ordering anything that included the word *deluxe*. And that really irked me. It always seemed that Bobby couldn't just order a plain cheeseburger; he had to have a "deluxe cheeseburger." Of course, that was always the most expensive one on the menu. And every week I would bawl him out about it, creating a "blue fog" over the entire luncheon gathering.

This was one of those times that, while there was no audible voice, it seemed that God and I carried on a conversation in my mind. He was asking me, "Bob, how much would you *like* Bobby to spend on lunch? What would make you happy?"

"I don't know, Lord. Maybe $2.25."

"Bob, how much is a 'deluxe cheeseburger'?"

"Well, about $2.75."

"How many times a year do you go out to lunch together?"

I thought, "I suppose about 50, if we went out every week."

"Why don't you figure out how much money that is."

I did. I got a piece of paper and multiplied out the difference between the lunch plates over a year. It came to about $25. I just stared at the paper. I felt ashamed and stupid. I didn't need an audible voice to know what the punch line of this conversation was.

"Bob, you are hurting the feelings of your son, whom you love more than anything in the world, and you are hurting your relationship with him over a measly $25 a year."

Without hesitation, I got up and drove home. I called Amy, Debbie, and Bobby together in the living room. "I've been spending some time with the Lord," I said, "and He showed me some things that I want to talk to you about. Especially with you, Bob.

"Do you know how I give you a hard time when we go out to lunch? How I say that 'you don't know what the right side of the menu is for'?" He nodded. "Bobby, when I yell at you because you order things that cost too much, does that hurt your feelings?" He didn't say anything, but big tears welled up in his eyes, and his lip began quivering.

"I had forgotten for a long time, but God reminded me this morning of something. When I was your age, my dad did the same thing to me. I didn't know what the right side of the menu was for, either! And it always hurt my feelings, too, and made those family dinners not quite as much fun as they should have been.

"Bobby, I want you to know I'm sorry. I love you very much, and I'm telling you now: If you want a deluxe cheeseburger, you can have a deluxe cheeseburger. And I am never going to bring it up again." We all hugged each other, and that was the end of the issue for good.

I'm sure that, to most other people, this is a trivial illustration. How important could a decision over a cheeseburger be? But the issue really isn't the cheeseburger or the menu. The issue is a love relationship. What law could ever have touched this situation? None, except the law of love.

The Greater Standard

When the Bible says that we aren't under the law anymore, it doesn't mean that we are left without standards. We are actually under a *higher* standard, called in the Scripture "the law of Christ" (Galatians 6:2) and "the law of liberty" (James 1:25 NASB).

Under grace, God says to us through the apostle Paul:

> You, my brothers, were called to be *free*. But do not use your freedom to indulge the flesh; rather, *serve one another in love*. The entire law is summed up in a single command: "Love your neighbor as yourself" (Galatians 5:13-14).

This is our standard, and it is indeed a *higher* standard than outward conformity to rules. Romans 13:10 sums it up: "Love does no harm to its neighbor. Therefore love is the fulfillment of the law."

It was Christ who said, "Do not think that I have come to abolish the law or the Prophets; I have not come to abolish them but to *fulfill them*" (Matthew 5:17). And He did fulfill the law: not by what He *did not* do, but by what He *did* do—He lived a life of perfect love.

The Lord Jesus Christ said, "All men will know that you are My disciples if you love one another" (John 13:35). There's only one way that it will ever happen: We must first receive God's love and grace—tune in to the "music"—or we'll have nothing to give. But if we will receive God's love and become channels of that love to others, we can walk in the assurance that we are fulfilling the highest purpose of God in our daily lives, because it was He Himself who said, "A new commandment I give you: Love one another. As I have loved you, so you must love one another" (John 13:34).

12

FREEDOM IN DEPENDENCY

George had been blind for most of his life due to a diabetic condition when he came to one of our training conferences a few years ago. He had endured several operations, and his fragile physical health was always a burden, but that wasn't the source of his greatest struggle. His greatest pain was emotional, coming from his belief that God had rejected him.

"Why do you feel that way?" I wanted to know. As George told me about his background and the teaching he had been under, I could hardly contain the flood of anger that came over me. The principle of "truth sets you free and error binds you" is no joke. Error was causing terrible pain to a sensitive and lovable young man who had enough real burdens in his life without adding to them with false teaching.

> He was taught that *the size of your faith* determines whether or not you can get from God what you are asking for. If you don't get it, who can you blame? Only yourself.

At his church, he told me, there was a great emphasis on faith. "If you have faith, you can do anything," was the attitude continually expressed. George's pastor would stand in the pulpit and say things like this: "If you get cancer and die, it's your own fault! You just don't have enough faith!"

But they didn't stop with ridiculous general pronouncements like that. Week after week as George entered the church service, someone would place a hymnal in his hands. Not by mistake—deliberately! Over and over in pious tones, the words were said, "Maybe today, George, you'll have enough faith to see. Maybe today you'll have the faith for God to heal you." But no matter how hard George tried to work up a lot of faith, he was never healed.

After "not having enough faith to see" for many years, George was a beaten, hopeless man. After all, he was taught that *the size of your faith* determines whether or not you can get from God what you are asking for. If you don't get it, who can you blame? Only yourself. And that's what he did. Obviously, God must hate him, he thought, because he was "a man of little faith."

⊷

Is that really what faith is all about? No, what George was taught was not faith at all. But he is certainly not alone. Many thousands of Christians are caught up in the same erroneous teaching that George was. Thousands of other people thrash around, having heard that "the Christian life is lived by faith," but don't have a clue how to do it.

I wrestled with it for years myself, even as I was confidently teaching other people about faith. I would quote Colossians 2:6 (NASB), "As you have received Christ Jesus the Lord, so walk in Him," and I would ask, "How did you receive Christ? By faith! Therefore, how are you to continue walking with Him? The same way—by faith!" I was right, but quite honestly I really didn't understand what I was talking about.

It is impossible to read the Bible even casually and miss the fact that faith is of crucial importance—especially when you come across statements like "Everything that does not come from faith is sin" (Romans 14:23), and "Without faith it is impossible to please God" (Hebrews 11:6). So we all agree how important it is to live by faith. But the nagging questions just won't go away: What does it *mean* to live by faith? And: How do you *do* it?

A Survey of Counterfeits

To begin, as with many other issues, it often helps to start with the counterfeits of the truth—in other words, what faith is *not*.

Faith Is Not a Feeling

As we saw in chapter 2, emotions are just responders to whatever we are thinking. Emotions come and go. The Bible speaks very little about what we should be *feeling*, but it has plenty to say about what we should be *doing*. Many people associate the tingly feelings they get in a stirring church service with faith. That's when they tend to make all kinds of resolutions and commitments to God. Reality sets in, however, when the service is over, the music stops, and they get in the car to go home. Since the stimulus is no longer there, the feelings fade away, too. The result of a dependency on religious feelings is a roller-coaster experience that leads to frustration and bondage. Exercising faith may *result* in feelings, but the feelings themselves are not faith.

Faith Is Not Intellectual Agreement with Doctrine

Sometimes we fall into the trap of just trying to get Christians to adhere to the same doctrinal positions. We begin believing that faith is a matter of the intellect. This is exactly the error that James is addressing in his letter: "You believe that there is one God. Good! Even the demons believe that—and shudder" (James 2.19). In one sense, even Satan has good doctrine! He knows who God is, he knows about the Trinity, and he knows that Jesus Christ died for our sins, rose again, and is seated at the Father's right hand. But is he in right relationship with God? No way. There is certainly an intellectual aspect to faith—you need true information to exercise faith—but intellectual agreement in itself is not faith.

The difference between intellectual belief and true faith is explained by a simple illustration I often use in teaching. Standing behind a podium, I point to a chair in the front row and say, "I can honestly tell you that I believe with all my heart that that chair will support me if I sit in it. Very seriously, there is not a shadow of doubt in my mind that that chair is trustworthy. That's the truth. *But I am not exercising what the Bible calls faith in that chair.* The word *faith* in the Bible includes the elements of *dependency* and *reliance.* Regardless of what I think intellectually, I am not doing what the Bible calls faith until I park my body down on it." So therefore, faith always involves a *decision of the will* to act on what the mind believes is true. Believing that the chair is capable of supporting me is not the same thing as actually sitting down in it. Faith always responds to the truth with action.

Faith Is Not a Power to Manipulate God

George's story is a perfect example of this error. What his teachers were calling "faith" was not faith at all. It was *presumption.* The difference is major. In true faith, God is always the initiator, and man is always the responder. In other words, God says something is true or makes a promise, and I respond by acting on it, depending on Him for the results. However, in presumption the order is reversed. Man assumes the role of initiator and tries to use "faith" as a power to force God to be the responder! The "red flags" that will warn you of presumption are when there is a lot of emphasis on faith as a "power" or when there is an emphasis on the *amount* of faith.

Faith's True Value

The truth is, *there is no power in faith itself. The value of faith is found only in its object.* Faith is like swallowing. Someone could say, "Swallowing enables you to live," and that sounds good at first. But you can also swallow and die! It's not swallowing that enables you to live; swallowing *food* enables you to live. But you can swallow poison and die, using the identical mechanism that you use to swallow food to live! In the same way, faith doesn't save us. Faith *in the Lord Jesus Christ* saves us!

Another way to look at it is by comparing faith to the clutch in a standard transmission car. Imagine that you own a fantastic new sports car, and you take me out for a spin. There we are, rocketing down the highway as you are showing off this amazing machine. I can hardly contain myself, and I exclaim, "I can't believe it! What a clutch! What a clutch!"

"What a clutch"? What would you think of me? You would think I was an idiot, wouldn't you? I'm not supposed to be admiring the clutch. I'm supposed to be admiring the powerful engine. There's no power in a clutch. The clutch is only what connects the power of the engine to the wheels. And that's what faith is like. There is no power in faith itself. *The power is God!* Faith is only that which connects the power of God to our humanity. That's why the size of our faith is not the issue. People often look at our ministry and say things like, "You must be a man of great faith." I tell them, "I don't have a great faith. I have a great God!" When you have a great God, you don't need a lot of faith—just enough to take Him at His word. That's why the Lord Jesus taught, "If you have faith as small as a mustard seed, you can say to this mulberry tree, 'Be uprooted and planted in the sea,' and it will obey you" (Luke 17:6).

The size of someone's faith is not important. What *is* important is the will of God. What the Lord is saying is that if it's God's will (as the initiator) that you move the tree, all it takes for you to move it (as the responder) is the faith to speak the command. The real question is always, "What has God said?" Our faith should be the same as that exemplified by Abraham, who was "fully assured that *what God had promised*, He was able also to perform" (Romans 4:21 NASB).

In the error that George was taught, God becomes virtually a genie in a bottle, who will do man's bidding if only he can learn the proper formulas. Presumption is really closer to magic than biblical faith.

Looking at the Author of Faith

I have been laying some foundational understanding to which we must hold accurately to even begin a discussion of living by faith. But for an example of how to put true faith into daily practice, we need look no farther than the Lord Jesus Himself. In my own life, coming to understand this truth was one of the most significant "missing puzzle pieces" that God fit together for me.

When I first came to Christ and for a long time afterward, the dominant truth in my mind was the fact that Jesus Christ is God. That truth had changed my life, and I held to it tenaciously. However, there were things I couldn't explain. One evening, a pair of Jehovah's Witnesses virtually wrapped me around a doorknob with objections to the deity of Christ. They asked questions like these: "If Jesus was God, who was He praying to? How did He get tired and hungry? For that matter, how can God die? There are verses in the gospels where Jesus says that the Father is greater than He, and there are places where Jesus says He didn't know some things. Now how can He be God?"

At the time, even though I knew the Scriptures regarding Christ's deity, I couldn't answer these questions. In my zeal to hold on to the truth of His deity, I failed to see clearly (and was even a little threatened by) His humanity. But the Bible is not at all timid in describing Christ's humanity. For example, 1 Corinthians 15:45,47 says:

> So it is written: "The first man Adam became a living being"; the last Adam, a life-giving spirit...The first man was of the dust of the earth, the second man from heaven.

Jesus, the True Man

Jesus always has been, is, and always will be God. His deity was never diminished one iota. I had that truth down. But I missed the fact that *on earth He didn't live as God*. During His 33 years on earth, He lived as the perfect *Man*, the Second Adam. Therefore, from God's point of view, Jesus Christ was the first true man to live on earth since Adam fell. Why? He possessed spiritual life. And being alive spiritually, He lived every day in total dependency upon His Father to live through Him. Every day Jesus presented His humanity to His Father as a vehicle to express the life of God to the world. As a result He could say, "Anyone who has seen Me has seen the Father" (John 14:9). For the first time in thousands of years, God could again be seen in a man!

To someone like me who had majored on the deity of Christ (and we should), it was a strange thought that Christ did not live on earth as God. But listen to His own words:

> Philip said, "Lord, show us the Father and that will be enough for us." Jesus answered: "Don't you know Me, Philip, even after I have been among you such a long time? Anyone who has seen Me has seen the Father. How can you say, 'Show us the Father'? Don't you believe that I am in the Father, and that the Father is

in Me? The words I say to you are not just My own. Rather, *it is the Father, living in Me, who is doing His work*" (John 14:8-10).

Without ever denying His deity, Jesus Christ lived on earth in exactly the same way that God intends every man to live. "But what about His miracles?" many people ask. The answer, as strange as it may sound at first, is that Jesus Christ never did a miracle simply because He was God, though God He certainly was. Every miracle performed by Christ was actually done by God the Father working through Him in His role as the perfect Man!

The Marvel of Total Dependency

Jesus' consistent attitude and testimony was, *"By Myself I can do nothing"* (John 5:30). He talked of "the very work that the Father has given Me to finish" (John 5:36). He explained, "For I did not speak of My own accord, but the Father who sent Me commanded Me what to say and how to say it" (John 12:49). Time and time again He emphasized that He was living a life of total dependency upon His Father.

What does this mean to you and me? The night before His crucifixion, Jesus told His disciples that, after His departure, He would send the Holy Spirit to them:

> And I will ask the Father, and He will give you another Counselor to be with you forever—the Spirit of truth. The world cannot accept Him, because it neither sees Him nor knows Him. But you know Him, for *He lives with you and will be in you.* I will not leave you as orphans; I will come to you...Because I live, you also will live (John 14.16-19).

The Lord went on to explain that by the Holy Spirit, *He would live in and through them in the same manner as the Father had lived in and through Him*: "On that day you will realize that I am in My Father, and *you are in Me, and I am in you*" (verse 20).

Jesus Christ laid down His life *for* us, so that He could give His life *to* us, so that He could live His life *through* us! That's the entire gospel in a nutshell. For 33 years He demonstrated the life of dependency (faith) that God had designed man for. Then He went to a cross, taking upon

Himself the punishment for our sins to settle the issue of our guilt before a holy God. But that's not all. He rose from the dead, and He now gives to anyone who believes that same resurrected life, restoring to men the ability to share in and express the life of God!

Following Christ, Our Pattern

The indwelling life of Christ is released in our daily experience when we live as He did, by faith—that is, with total dependency upon the God who lives in us. But "a life of total dependency" is an elusive concept for people to grasp. The best explanation I have heard has been expressed by Major Ian Thomas in what he calls the "threefold interlock." A life of faith is *our love for God,* resulting in *dependency upon God,* resulting in *obedience to God.*

This pattern is clearly seen in the life of Jesus Christ. The first and greatest commandment of the law was, "Love the Lord your God with all your heart and with all your soul and with all your mind" (Matthew 22:37). Only Christ ever fulfilled the commandment. Every moment of His earthly life, Jesus loved His Father. As a result of that *love,* He lived the life of total *dependency* that we have already seen: "By Myself I can do nothing" (John 5:30). His attitude of perfect surrender could only result in a life of perfect *obedience,* crowned in the Garden of Gethsemane where, even in the approaching horror of the cross and His taking upon Himself our sins, He prayed, "Father, if You are willing, take this cup from Me; *yet not My will, but Yours be done*" (Luke 22:42).

> Most Christian teaching through history and today has been directed at getting Christians to live obediently, while ignoring the necessity of love and dependency.

As beloved children, we are called to live according to the same pattern as the Lord Jesus: *love for* God, resulting in *dependency upon* God, resulting in *obedience to* God. It is only as we approach the Christian life in this order that we will be experiencing the true freedom and life that God has purposed for us, and it's the only way we will be truly obeying God according to His will. Unfortunately though, most Christian teaching throughout history and today has been directed at getting Christians to live obediently, while ignoring the necessity of love and dependency. It can never work.

Love *and* Dependency

Apart from a heart that is truly learning to love God, we will have no *motivation* for obedience other than abject fear of punishment. On the other hand, apart from an understanding of what it means to live dependently—that is, by faith—we will have no *ability* to live obediently, and we will be set up for a "Romans 7 experience": "For what I want to do I do not do, but what I hate I do" (Romans 7:15). A lack of understanding in either of these areas—love as our motivation or dependency as our source of power—leads inevitably to a return to the law. If you have ever wondered why Christians' lives and morality often don't rise above the world's level, this is the reason. Apart from God's pattern, we have no motivation or power for true obedience.

All right, then how do we learn to love God? That's what this whole book is about. As I have spelled out in many ways, we have no ability in ourselves to produce love for God, regardless of how much we would like to or feel we should. The Bible makes it plain. "This is love: *not that we loved God, but that He loved us* and sent His Son as the one who would turn aside His wrath, taking away our sins" (1 John 4:10, alternate rendering). *We must first receive God's unconditional love and acceptance for us before we will ever learn to love Him in return.* "We love because He first loved us" (1 John 4:19).

It is the message of God's unconditional love and grace—total forgiveness, righteousness, acceptance, and life—that He freely gives us in Jesus Christ that transforms hearts and lives.

> For if, by the trespass of the one man [Adam], death reigned through that one man, *how much more will those who receive God's abundant provision of grace and of the gift of righteousness reign in life through the one man, Jesus Christ* (Romans 5:17).

That is our motivation.

Where does our power come from? Jesus used a simple illustration to describe our life in Him: "I am the vine, you are the branches; he who abides in Me and I in him, he bears much fruit, for apart from Me you can do nothing" (John 15:5 NASB). Jesus said that He is the vine and we are branches. Think about the role of a branch. Does a branch *produce* fruit or does a branch *bear* fruit? It *bears* fruit! If you cut a branch off the vine and laid it on the ground, how much fruit would come from it? None. There is no power in a branch to produce the fruit; it's just a "fruit-hanger." However, a branch can bear tremendous amounts of fruit by just doing what it was created to do: by abiding in the vine and allowing the life of the vine to flow through it.

Notice some other things about branches that are abiding in the vine. They aren't working hard. They aren't getting "burned out." They aren't considering "giving up the vineyard." As a matter of fact, they aren't even concentrating on *themselves* at all, nor on *fruit*. It wouldn't do any good, anyway. The branches are totally dependent on the vine to do the producing. The only preoccupation of a branch should be the moment-by-moment receiving of the life of the vine.

What does that tell you about the Christian life? You and I are not responsible for *producing* the Christian life! We aren't *able* to produce the Christian life—only Christ can produce it. Our responsibility is to maintain a dependent, receiving attitude—the same attitude of availability that Jesus presented to His Father for 33 years—and Christ will produce the fruit of His life in us; those same qualities that are called the "fruit of the Spirit" in Galatians 5:22-23. It comes through an attitude that says, "Lord, I can't—but You can."

Surrender and Renewal

Christians of all camps agree that obedience to God is the desired goal. It is the *means* of getting that obedience—the question, "How are you going to do it?"—that becomes the problem. God has made it clear in His Word that legalistic obedience without a surrendered heart is worthless to Him. Jesus twice quoted Hosea 6:6: "For I desire mercy, not sacrifice, and acknowledgment of God rather than burnt offerings." Both cases were in response to those who focused on keeping the letter of the law, but totally missed the spirit behind it. Through the apostle Paul, God tells us the true way:

Therefore, I urge you, brothers, in view of of God's mercy, to *offer your bodies as living sacrifices*, holy and pleasing to God— which is your spiritual worship. Do not conform any longer to the pattern of this world, but *be transformed by the renewing of your mind*. Then you will be able to test and approve what God's will is—His good, pleasing and perfect will (Romans 12:1-2).

Paul is describing an attitude of total surrender. The motivation he offers is "in view of God's mercy." What's that? The love and grace of God that he has been discussing for 11 chapters! Now, he says, the most reasonable, logical thing you can do is to offer yourselves without reserve to a God who loves you beyond comprehension.

Notice that he isn't talking about commitment. Commitment and surrender are two different things. Commitment is what I am promising to do for God. Surrender is placing myself and my life in His hands to do with as He pleases. It's like those old World War I movies. Furious trench warfare is going on, with bombs exploding and machine guns crackling. Then a small white flag is raised on a stick and waved from a trench. "We give up," they're saying. "Do with us whatever you please. We're sick and tired of being sick and tired." That total release of giving up everything is what Paul is telling us. But we aren't surrendering ourselves to an enemy! We are surrendering ourselves to a loving God and Father, who will take charge of our lives in His perfect wisdom and control. Why would we ever hesitate, once we have learned of His love for us?

After exhorting us to adopt this attitude, the first thing Paul mentions is, "Be transformed by the renewing of your mind." In other words, allow God to begin teaching your mind His truth to replace the error of natural thinking. Based on His Word, begin to look at yourself and life from God's perspective, rather than from man's perspective. That's why I have discussed so extensively the believer's identity in Christ. Knowing who you are is essential. You have to know that you're a "butterfly" before it makes any sense to think about flying.

Dependency Expressed in Thankfulness

One of the most fundamental things that we are surrendering to Christ is *all claim to personal rights*. Now I'm not talking about civil rights, like the right to vote. I'm talking about things we tend to demand from life—things like a right to happiness, the right to be noticed, the right for life to be fair, the right to be appreciated, the right to get my own way.

There's a very simple reason why this must be so: *You can't hold on to rights and maintain a thankful spirit at the same time.* The essence of a life of faith is a thankful heart. That is a thread that runs through the entire Bible, Old and New Testaments. It is expressed concisely in a single verse, 1 Thessalonians 5:18: "Give thanks in all circumstances, for this is God's will for you in Christ Jesus."

Many times I find myself counseling someone who is all bent out of shape in anxiety over a decision. "What is God's will for me in this situation?" they ask.

"I don't know for sure what God's will is in regard to your situation," I answer, "but I do know this: It's God's will that you *give thanks* in this situation."

Why would God tell us to give thanks in all circumstances, even in bad ones? Because giving thanks is a concrete expression of our faith in God—that our lives are in His hands, and that we are trusting Him to fulfill His promise in Romans 8:28: "And we know that in all things God works for the good of those who love Him, who have been called according to His purpose." The result of trusting God with our lives and expressing that faith through giving thanks is a freedom and peace that is supernatural:

> Do not be anxious about anything, but in everything, by prayer and petition, *with thanksgiving*, present your requests to God. And the peace of God, which transcends all understanding, will guard your hearts and your minds in Christ Jesus (Philippians 4:6-7).

The greatest example I have witnessed of this truth in action was the story of a young couple named Reed and Marian. Reed was one of several fathers taking a girls' group on a camping trip to Oklahoma. Before leaving their home in Dallas, their six-year-old daughter, Wendy, came up and asked, "Mommy, is it okay if I ride in the other car with my friend? She doesn't have anybody to ride with." Marian said it was fine, and the group set out. It was raining and the streets were slick. Before the group had gotten far, the driver of the car in which Wendy was riding lost control. He tried to bring the vehicle back, but the trailer they were hauling fishtailed. They crashed across the median and into the lane of oncoming traffic. Miraculously, in a chain-reaction accident that eventually totalled 26 cars, the most serious injury was a broken arm to one of the girls—that is, except for Wendy. Wendy was thrown out of the car and was instantly killed.

Just a few weeks later, I was riding with Reed in a funeral limousine. This time, he was a pallbearer for one of his closest friends, Steve, who had died of cancer at the age of 32. Surprisingly though, Reed was his usual soft-spoken, smiling self, even though his eyes were teary. In spite of everything, he seemed to be doing very well.

"Well, Reed," I said gently, "I suppose you have had enough of this to last you for a while."

He smiled and said, "That's for sure."

"Tell me," I asked. "How are you holding up? How have you learned to deal with the loss of Wendy?"

"Let me tell you about that," he said. "Marian and I look at it this way. What if God had come to us six years ago and made us an offer: 'Reed and Marian, I have a little girl, a daughter of Mine, named Wendy. Now she's only going to be on earth for six years. But I need someone who will love her, look after her, and teach her about Me for those six years. Then I'm going to take her home to Me. So I wonder: Would you like Me to give her to you, realizing that those are the conditions?' Marian and I both would have said, 'Oh yes, Lord. Give her to us!'

"And that's just what we feel that God has done. He always knew that Wendy would only be on earth for six years. We have chosen to be thankful for every one of those six years that Wendy enriched our lives. We miss her terribly. We've cried, and we'll cry more tears. But we know that we'll see her again, and we thank God for it all."

What an attitude! In the face of great loss, a thankful heart. A thankful heart that has surrendered all rights to a sovereign, loving God. Because of their response of faith, that young couple has lived at peace ever since. A tragedy? Yes! But they have discovered the reality of Romans 8:38-39:

For I am convinced that neither death nor life, neither angels
nor demons, neither the present nor the future, nor any pow-
ers, neither height nor depth, nor anything else in all creation,
will be able to separate us from the love of God that is in Christ
Jesus our Lord.

⁓≋⁓

I shared this story with George. He, too, made the decision to give
thanks, in total surrender to the Lord who loved him and promised to
cause even his blindness to work together for good. At that conference
George found genuine peace, and 18 months later he went to be with
the Lord. His mother wrote to me afterward. George's feelings, she said,
were that "the last 18 months were worth it all" because of what he had
learned about the reality of Christ. Through placing his total dependency
upon Jesus Christ, George found Him to be all He claimed to be—the
answer to every need of the human heart.

13

GROWING IN GRACE

It's been many years since the day I was driving down the expressway with tears streaming down my cheeks, crying out to God to restore to me the joy of my salvation.

My prayer at the time was, "Lord, take me back to the days when I first knew You." I had no idea how God was going to answer that prayer. The funny thing is, I'm glad He didn't do what I asked! *Today I wouldn't want to go back.* Today I know so much more about His love and grace and about what it means to be alive in Christ, that I would never want to return to where I was as a new Christian. The answer did not lie in going *back*; the answer was to go *forward*.

It reminds me of the story of Israel after Moses led them through the Red Sea. It was never God's intention that they linger in the desert. He told them to go right ahead into the Promised Land, where they could eat from trees they did not plant and drink from wells they did not dig. But because of their unbelief, they would not enter into the rest to which God had called them. Afraid to go ahead and unable to return to Egypt, the desert was all they had left, with its boredom, monotony, and dryness. As the reality of their situation started to sink in, the people began complaining about Moses' leadership. Incredibly, they even started to fondly recall the "good old days" in Egypt! Moses reminded them of the fact that they were beaten-down slaves in Egypt, but that made no impact on them. Even slavery looks good to you when you're living in the desert.

When we as Christians are not willing to enter into the Sabbath rest we are called to—resting totally in the truth of God's unconditional love and grace in Jesus Christ—we are behaving just like the Israelites. We are Christians, and we can't go back and become lost again, anymore than butterflies can go back and become worms again. We won't go forward either, so we make our home in the desert and settle for second best. Now, if you're going to live in the desert, you might as well make it as comfortable and enjoyable as possible, and that's just what we have done.

The Christian world that we have fashioned reminds me of a real city in the desert—Las Vegas, Nevada. If you think about it, there isn't any special reason for Las Vegas to even exist. But taking advantage of the legal gambling in Nevada, people have made that city a mecca for vacationers. As far as the world is concerned, they have built the flashiest, most exciting playground in America—right in the middle of the desert, in a place that no one would ever visit otherwise, let alone live. If your intention is to excite and gratify the flesh, Las Vegas is just about the most comfortable and entertaining place you can imagine.

> For a while, I was very content with all the glitz and flashy show-biz approach to the Christian life…I am so thankful today that God allowed me to go through that desert experience until I was totally sick and tired of it.

Like a "spiritual Las Vegas," the Christian world has built "Tinseltown in the Desert." It looks pretty on the surface, but it's nine miles wide and one inch deep. It's flashy, it's sometimes exciting, and it will keep you occupied—for a while. But every now and then, a small voice in our hearts begins asking, "Is this really what the Lord Jesus had in mind when He talked about an 'abundant life'?" For a while, I was very content with all the glitz and flashy show-biz approach to the Christian life. But after a time it became old. I grew cynical and burned-out because it was just a performance. I am so thankful today that God allowed me to go through that desert experience until I was totally sick and tired of it. He then answered my cry and brought me to a newness of life that I never could have imagined.

Resting and Growing

God has always had a remnant that has said, "Lord, I'm *not* satisfied with the same old thing. I don't want to practice a religion; I want to know You in a real relationship." To the hungry ones, to the humble ones, God will always respond by leading them into true freedom. Jesus gave us the assurance: "Ask and it will be given to you; seek and you will find; knock and the door will be opened to you" (Matthew 7:7). And we can do this knowing that God "is able to do immeasurably more than all we ask or imagine, according to His power that is at work within us" (Ephesians 3:20).

The writer of Hebrews describes this life as a "Sabbath-rest." In the beginning, God created everything in six days, "so on the seventh day He rested from all His work" (Genesis 2:2). In Hebrews 4:9-10 the spiritual meaning of this pattern is explained: "There remains, then, a Sabbath-rest for the people of God; for anyone who enters *God's rest* also rests from his own work, just as God did from His." In other words, God wants us to grasp by faith the fact that Jesus Christ has done it all, and there is nothing left for us to perform to be acceptable to God. In other words, "God has done the work; now *you* rest!"

Realize, though, that "resting" is not the same thing as being *inactive*. I can't think of anyone more *active* than the Lord Jesus Christ, but He was always at rest. At rest in our hearts, we are strongly urged in the Word of God to go forward aggressively and lay hold of all that God has prepared for us. *We are called to grow in grace!*

The exhortation to grow in grace is a consistent theme in the New Testament. A life of faith is not passive; it requires a firm decision of the will and perseverance to believe God and His Word as your *only* standard of truth and proceed to apply faith to everyday life. The apostle Paul urged us to "continue to work out your salvation with fear and trembling [a spirit of humility], for it is *God who works in you* to will and to act according to his good purpose" (Philippians 2:12-13). Notice that it doesn't say "work *for* your salvation." It says "work *out* your salvation." As verse 13 makes clear, it is *God* in us who is initiating *His* work. Our role is to work *out* with all our strength what God is working *in*.

Making Yourself Available

God doesn't need your *ability*. *He* is the able one. He needs your *availability*; that is, making your body totally available to Jesus Christ just as He made His own body totally available to His Father 2000 years ago. When we learn this secret, we may work harder than ever, but we don't become burned-out. Remember that it was Christ Himself who said,

> Come to Me, all you who are weary and burdened, and I will give you *rest*. Take My yoke upon you and learn from Me, for I am gentle and humble in heart, and you will find *rest* for your souls. For My yoke is easy and My burden is light (Matthew 11:28-30).

People do not end up in a counselor's office, nor do they become fanatical, judgmental, or self-righteous through carrying the yoke of Jesus! Taking on the yoke of Jesus means becoming His willing disciple, that is, a lifelong learner. It means totally trusting Him with our lives. It may mean difficulty; it may mean facing rejection; it may mean a great deal of hard work—*but it will not burn you out*. The yoke of Jesus also means rest, peace, and fulfillment in a life linked with His.

The first reason we don't become burned-out is because we are not acting *contrary* to our real identities. We are merely living out who we are: new creatures in Christ! "Therefore, if anyone is in Christ, he is a new creation; the old has gone, the new has come!" (2 Corinthians 5:17). We have become "partakers of the divine nature" (2 Peter 1:4 NASB), and "we have the mind of Christ" (1 Corinthians 2:16). We don't feel a conflict with the moving of the Spirit in our lives (though the flesh may resist). Our souls experience the greatest peace and harmony imaginable when we are responding to the urgings of God through the Holy Spirit.

The second reason that we don't burn out is because we are not producing the life on our own; Christ Himself is producing His life in and through us. "To this end I labor, struggling with all *His energy, which so powerfully works in me*" (Colossians 1:29). It is truly a miraculous lifestyle! A total mystery to the world, but revealed to and experienced by God's people who have received the incredible message, "Christ in you, the hope of glory" (Colossians 1:27). Christ living through us is God's only solution for man to be restored to the intelligent purpose for which he was made—to be a living vehicle for God to express His life to all creation!

Christ living in us is the only thing that will fulfill the deepest need in the heart of man—the need for meaning and purpose in life.

The Privilege of Letting God Work Through You

Imagine yourself one day receiving a phone call from the president of the United States. "How are you?" he asks, just as if you were old friends, and you chat for a while. "By the way," he goes on, "I'm going to be in town the day after tomorrow, and I need the use of a car. I wonder if I could use yours?"

You know how you would respond. The next day, you would be out washing and waxing that car. You would vacuum and scrub the interior. You would go over it with a fine-tooth comb. If you happened to talk to any friends, you would find a way to work into the conversation a casual comment such as, "Well, I don't know about going shopping. After all, the president will be using my car tomorrow..."

Then the big day comes when the president of the United States borrows your car—maybe the proudest day of your life. Afterward, you would make a shrine out of that vehicle. You might even have a brass plaque made: "The president of the United States drove this car" with the date underneath. If it were at all possible, you would find a way to keep that car in mint condition. Who knows? Maybe you could donate it to the Smithsonian!

I know I'm overdoing it a bit, but I share this illustration for a reason. We think it would be a great honor to serve for one day a man who holds an elected office in our country, and it would be. *But we Christians hardly consider the fact that the God who created this universe lives in us and wants to use our bodies every day of our lives!* Think about it. If you are a Christian, God lives in you and wants to produce fruit through you that will endure for eternity! "For we are God's workmanship, created in Christ Jesus to do good works, which God prepared in advance for us to do" (Ephesians 2:10). I can't think of a better reason to approach life with contagious enthusiasm.

Points of Resistance

In spite of the fact that it is full of good news, classic Christianity is resisted and met with objections by many people. This is where we begin to run into the "buts" and "what abouts?" "I know we're under grace, *but...*" "I know we're totally forgiven, *but...*" "I know Christ lives in us, *but...*" That's when we become what I call "billy-goat Christians": *but, but, but.* We are simply afraid to believe that God really means what He says.

Pressure or Desire?

Bible study and prayer are two issues that are brought up repeatedly. Recently, a man asked me, "But if you don't keep people under the law, how do you get them to study their Bibles? How do you get them to pray?" He was honestly bewildered. I knew that his background included a great deal of Bible study and Scripture memorization, but to him these were "disciplines." His working assumption was that Christians *don't* want to do these things, and that they need to be firmly pressured to do them.

"Let me ask you a question," I countered. "Did you ever get a letter from someone you were in love with? Did anyone have to tell you to read it? If you are like everyone else I've ever met, you read it over and over, backward and forward, and between the lines! When you're in love, nobody has to tell you to act that way. You just do it.

"When I was a new Christian and ever since, no one had to tell me to read my Bible. I *wanted* to do it. I love the Lord, and it's exciting to read His 'love letter' to me. Besides, I can't stand the thought of living *without* the Word, because it's my spiritual food. Jesus said, 'Man does not live on bread alone, but on every word that comes from the mouth of God' (Matthew 4:4). I read my Bible for the same reason that I *eat*: because I'm *hungry!*

"Here's an illustration," I continued. "If I were a doctor, and someone came to me and said this: 'Doc, I have absolutely no appetite for food. I don't mean once in a while; I mean *ever*'; I would immediately know, *There's something wrong with this man.* Fluctuations in appetite are normal, but absolutely no appetite is a sign of sickness, and I would try to find out what it is! And that's exactly the way I respond to a Christian who tells me that he has no desire at all to read the Bible—or that he has no desire to pray or assemble with other believers. That's not normal; that's *abnormal*—a sign of bondage brought about by error. So

I would try to identify the error and replace it with truth from the Word of God.

"Just like my physical appetite, my spiritual appetite ebbs and flows. It isn't perfectly consistent, and I don't worry about it if the fluctuations aren't extreme. But there are times, physically, when I get the flu and have no appetite for food at all. Then I'll often have to force myself to eat, knowing that I need to keep my strength up. In the same way, there are times when I might not have a desire for God's Word, and the reason is because I have started believing the lie of legalism and the accusations of the Accuser. At those times, even though I don't have the desire, I'll make myself get into the Bible simply because I know I need to renew my mind with truth. But don't forget, those times are still the abnormal, not the normal state of my spiritual life. My assumption is that when a man understands the fullness of God's love and acceptance, he'll *want* to read God's Word; he'll *want* to spend time with his heavenly Father in prayer; and he'll *want* to gather with other believers for worship and encouragement."

Complicating Life Under the Law of Love

Learning a new approach to decision-making also confuses many people. Actually, they become confused because they tend to make it far more complicated than it is. When I face a specific situation in life, I find that decisions are fairly simple when I know that "it is no longer I who live, but Christ lives in me" (Galatians 2:20 NASB). I have already made the larger decision of Romans 12:1 to present my body as a living sacrifice to God. I have already yielded my will and my personal rights to God, and I have already adopted the Word of God as my authority and standard of truth.

Therefore, decisions are determined by the law of love!

> For *the love of Christ controls us*, having concluded this, that one died for all, therefore all died; and He died for all, so that they who live *might no longer live for themselves, but for Him* who died and rose again on their behalf" (2 Corinthians 5:14-15 NASB).

Therefore, with the *motivation* of the love of Christ, the *decision* to present myself to Him for His use, and the *knowledge* from the Word of what God's will is in this specific situation, *I merely do by faith what the Bible says and leave the results to Him.*

Am I worried about a problem? When I understand that God is sovereign over all events, a problem becomes an opportunity to trust the Lord. I don't know what will happen tomorrow, but I do know one thing: The same Jesus who is in my today is already there! So, *controlled by the love of Christ,* I claim the promise of Philippians 4:6-7:

> Do not be anxious about anything, but in everything, by prayer and petition, with thanksgiving, present your requests to God. And the peace of God, which transcends all understanding, will guard your hearts and your minds in Christ Jesus.

I pray about the problem, give thanks, and leave the results to God. The result is an experience of that supernatural peace which is not dependent upon circumstances.

Am I angry and out of sorts with another person? The Bible says,

> Get rid of all bitterness, rage and anger, brawling and slander, along with every form of malice. Be kind and compassionate to one another, forgiving each other, just as in Christ God forgave you (Ephesians 4:31-32).

Therefore, *controlled by the love of Christ,* I go to the person I have offended to try to be reconciled and settle the issue. How will *he* respond? I don't know. The Scripture says, "If it is possible, *as far as it depends on you,* live at peace with everyone" (Romans 12:18). The results are in God's hands but, *motivated by His love,* I can act according to His will: "Do not be overcome by evil, but overcome evil with good" (Romans 12:21).

Am I out of work, and tempted to steal? God says, "He who has been stealing must steal no longer, but must work, doing something useful with his own hands, that he may have something to share with those in need" (Ephesians 4:28). Jesus said, "But seek first His kingdom and His righteousness, and all these things [your needs] will be given to you as well" (Matthew 6:33). Therefore, *motivated by the love of Christ,* I trust God to fulfill that promise to supply my needs as I go out and apply for a new job—not only so that I can be fed, but so that I can serve other people, provide for my family, and help perpetuate the work of the Lord through my finances. I get into action, trusting in His promise that "my God will meet all your needs according to *His* glorious riches in Christ Jesus" (Philippians 4:19). The Christian life is not nearly as complicated as we try to make it!

A License to Sin?

A frequently asked question is, "Will some believers take the message of grace as a license to sin?" I answer it this way: "If their understanding of the gospel goes no farther than the forgiveness of sins—probably yes. But when you understand that Christ not only died for the forgiveness of your sins, but also rose again to come and live in you—absolutely not!" There are those who, because of immaturity or rebellion, try to presume on grace for a while; but anyone who tries living according to the flesh will discover that real, abundant life is not found there—in fact, he will probably be even more miserable than when he was lost. If Christ lives in you, you can't live a lawless life without tremendous internal conflict. If you are a butterfly, you will never be happy living with the worms again! And since God is committed to conforming His children to the image of Christ, He can be counted on to apply appropriate, loving discipline to get them back on track.

> If Christ lives in you, you can't live a lawless life without tremendous internal conflict. If you are a butterfly, you will never be happy living with the worms again!

Understanding the Difference Between Discipline and Punishment

Notice that I said "discipline" and not "punishment." Though those terms are often thought to mean the same thing, they are very different. The confusion of the two concepts probably comes from our experiences with well-meaning but fallible human parents, who often disciplined us in love, but also sometimes punished us in frustration and anger. We then project those characteristics upon God, and assume that He acts the same way. However, nothing could be farther from the truth. This error is one of the final strongholds of legalism that must be corrected in order to enable a person to rest in God's grace. Let's begin by getting a proper definition of the terms.

Punishment is a penalty imposed on an offender for a crime or wrongdoing. It has retribution in view (paying someone back what he deserves) rather than correction. Punishment is looking *backward* to the offense, is *impersonal* and *automatic*, and its goal is the administration of *justice*. The simplest example of punishment in action is the policeman who pulls you over and gives you a ticket for speeding. Have you ever had that happen to you? I did recently when I was driving down the freeway. I didn't intend to speed. I was just preoccupied and wasn't paying attention to the speed limit. I try to be a law-abiding citizen. I explained all that to the police officer and, I must say, he was very sympathetic and understanding—as he wrote out that ticket.

You see, the law officer isn't interested in why you were speeding; he doesn't care whether or not you did it on purpose; nor is he interested in hearing about all the other days that you did abide by the law. All he knows is that you broke the law, and here is your penalty. You will also notice that he did nothing to compliment the 50 other drivers he saw that were within the speed limit. He just sat there, unresponsive, until there was a violation, then he got into action. That's punishment.

Discipline, on the other hand, is totally different. Discipline is *training* that develops self-control, character, and ability. It is looking *forward* to a beneficial result, is very *personal*, and is in *continuous* exercise. Back in high school, I played on the basketball team. We had a coach who worked us hard. He made us run laps. He made us run up and down bleachers. He made us run basketball drills and plays over and over until sometimes I thought my legs would drop off. Why did he make us do all those things? *Because he wanted us to succeed!* He didn't do those things because he was angry with us; he did them so that we would be good players and a well-prepared team.

One thing you will notice immediately, especially if you ever had a coach like mine, is that punishment and discipline sometimes *feel* the same to the one on the receiving end! But the sharp difference can be seen in both the *attitude* and the *goal* of the one doing it. The attitude behind punishment is *anger* and *indignation*, and its goal is *justice*; the attitude behind discipline is *love*, and its goal is the *benefit* and *development* of the person.

A total contrast! And the crucial application to us is knowing that *God, under the New Covenant, never deals with His children on the basis of punishment*. All of the punishment of God for our sins was fully received by our Savior Jesus Christ on the cross. *Now that we are children of God, He deals with us only on the basis of discipline*, which, once you understand the difference, is an extremely positive truth! He is not dealing with us in anger, nor with a demand for justice. He deals with us as a loving Father who is committed to His beloved children and to teaching them to grow in grace.

Receiving Discipline Means You're His Child

This issue is one that we will have to settle for two reasons. First, because Jesus said, "In this world you will have trouble" (John 16:33). Second, because, when faced with the tragedies and troubles of life, there is no human tendency stronger than to ask the question, "Why?" "Why did this happen?" we cry. "Is this problem a sign that God is angry with me?"

A tremendous illustration of this principle came to Tim Stevenson one day when he was out running on some country roads. "I had a trip planned that I was really excited about," Tim explains. "I was going on a week-long wilderness canoe trip to Canada, to an area that I had been to several times before and really love. But this was no leisurely vacation. This part of Canada is true wilderness. It's very challenging, so I was spending several weeks getting ready for the trip—running extra miles, doing some extra push-ups, and so on.

"This particular day, it was about 90 degrees in the Texas sun, with the heat radiating off the blacktop roads. I had nearly completed my three-mile run, dead-tired, when an idea suddenly occurred to me. If my body could talk, I thought, it would be saying, 'What is this? What's going on? Why are you doing this to me? Are you mad at me? Is there some unconfessed sin in my life?'

"I would have answered back, 'Body, I'm not mad at you. I'm doing this because I love you. I know the future and you don't. I know that in about six weeks, you're going to be paddling a canoe for up to eight hours a day; you're going to be carrying a 75-pound canoe or a 90-pound food pack for up to a mile at a time, up and down hills, often through sloppy mud. You'll have a whole week of that. Now, if I get you ready, you'll have a great time. If I don't get you ready, you are going to die.'

"I burst out laughing as I realized that this is exactly how we respond to God when we run into problems. Like the ancient pagans, we are continually trying to interpret events. When things go our way, it means the gods are happy with us; when we run into problems, it means the gods are angry with us. That's the way man naturally thinks, and we still carry that into the Christian life. We still find it hard to trust in the good intentions of a God who has done everything conceivable to demonstrate His love and concern for us!"

Responding to Life's Difficulties

This tendency to doubt God in times of trouble is exactly the real meaning of a passage on discipline often taken out of context, Hebrews 12:1-11. In this passage we are told to "endure hardship as discipline; God is treating you as sons. For what son is not disciplined by his father?" (Hebrews 12:7). Our response to this passage will be determined by the clarity of our understanding of discipline and punishment. The Hebrews, to whom the letter is addressed, were Jewish Christians who were facing tremendous pressures and trials. They were being barred from the temple and synagogues, they were being ostracized and threatened, and many were wavering in their faith. They were beginning to ask the same questions that we ask today: "Why are these things happening? Is it a sign that God has rejected us?" The writer of this letter wrote to encourage them, "No, God has not rejected you. Don't give up. Keep on going."

That's why chapter 11 of Hebrews was written. It has been called "God's Hall of Faith." The writer shows example after example of individuals who have trusted God throughout biblical history. He talks of those

> who through faith conquered kingdoms, administered justice, and gained what was promised; who shut the mouths of lions, quenched the fury of the flames, and escaped the edge of the sword; whose weakness was turned to strength; and who became powerful in battle and routed foreign armies. Women received back their dead, raised to life again (Hebrews 11:33-35).

That sure sounds exciting! Who wouldn't want to be a hero of the faith when those are the results? But unfortunately, we tend to stop reading in just the wrong place. The passage goes on:

> Others were tortured and refused to be released, so that they might gain a better resurrection. Some faced jeers and flogging, while still others were chained and put in prison. They were stoned; they were sawed in two; they were put to death by the sword. They went about in sheepskins and goatskins, destitute, persecuted and mistreated—the world was not worthy of them. They wandered in deserts and mountains, and in caves and holes in the ground (Hebrews 11:35-38).

Some heroes of the faith won battles; some heroes of the faith were killed; but "these were *all* commended for their faith" (Hebrews 11:39).

Trusting in His Total Acceptance

Instead of being like the ancient pagans who interpreted all negative experiences as being evidence of the displeasure of "the gods," we can look at tribulations according to truth. James wrote, "Consider it *pure joy*, my brothers, whenever you face trials of many kinds" (James 1:2). Paul said the same thing and told us the reason why:

> We also *rejoice in our sufferings*, because we know that suffering produces perseverance; perseverance, *character*; and character, hope. And hope does not disappoint us, because God has poured out His love into our hearts by the Holy Spirit, whom He has given us (Romans 5:3-5).

You and I are going to face trouble in the future. That's part of life in this fallen world. God does not promise us an exemption from tribulation, but He does promise that He will go with us through it. He does promise to cause "all things to work together for good to those who love God, to those who are called according to His purpose" (Romans 8:28 NASB). He does promise that if we get off the track in our Christian life, He will apply loving corrective discipline to restore us. He does promise that we can experience His peace and joy in the midst of our trials through trusting Him in an attitude of thanksgiving. Finally, He promises us that nothing that happens to us is a sign of His rejection. We can accept any personal tribulation as a discipline: an opportunity for God to build into us character qualities that are of eternal value.

Whatever your future holds, you can rest assured that "He who began a good work in you will carry it on to completion until the day of Christ Jesus" (Philippians 1:6). You may not know what will happen to you tomorrow, but you *can* know that the same Christ who loves you perfectly today is already there.

WHATEVER HAPPENED
TO THE REAL THING?

Sharon called me on *People to People* one night. "I've really benefited from your teaching," she said, "and I'm learning more and more about God's love for me. But I have a situation that I don't know what to do with." She paused and took a deep breath.

"I'm nineteen years old now, but when I was young and into my teens, I was sexually molested by four of my uncles. Since then I've come to know Jesus, and I don't hate them anymore. I've forgiven them. But the problem is that we have these family reunions where I see all of them, and I don't know how to handle it."

What can you say on live nationwide radio to a question like this? All I know to do is to trust in God and His Word. "Sharon," I said, "my heart just breaks for you. That's such a terrible thing...it's even hard for me to imagine such a background. I'm so thankful that you have come to know Christ, and that He's healing you of the hurt and bitterness that are natural to feel after experiences like yours."

I paused for a moment. "But after all that, Sharon, as much as I may empathize with you, there's really only one issue that matters right now—what will you do *today*? There's nothing you or I or anyone else can do to change the past. The question is, What will you do today and in the future? God promised us in Romans 8:28, 'And we know that in all things God works for the good of those who love Him, who have been called according to His purpose.' Now, it didn't say that all things *look* good, or that all things *feel* good, or even that all things *are* good. It's saying that God will cause all things *to work together* for good. I know that's hard to understand, but let's work through it.

"Think about this, Sharon," I continued. "Do you think you'll run into any other women in your life who have been through similar experiences?"

"I'm sure I will," she answered softly, her voice breaking as she tried not to cry.

> "Sharon, you can have a thankful heart for a God…who will take even terrible experiences like yours and turn them into an opportunity for good, as you go free in your own spirit."

"I think so, too, Sharon," I said. "How many do you think?"

"I don't know," Sharon responded, "maybe hundreds."

"In this sinful, sad world, that's probably true," I said. "Sharon, the best possible person in the world to minister to those women with the love and compassion of Jesus is *somebody who's been there.* You see, Sharon, we're called to be servants, just like Christ was. But in order to be an effective servant, we have to have compassion. How do we learn compassion? There's only one way I know of—by going through trials and tribulations ourselves. That's why we read in 2 Corinthians 1:3-4, 'Praise be to the God and Father of our Lord Jesus Christ, *the Father of compassion* and the God of all comfort, who comforts us in all our troubles, *so that we can comfort those in any trouble with the comfort we ourselves have received from God.'*

"You see, *there's* a reason for you to apply the command to 'give thanks in all circumstances' (1 Thessalonians 5:18). Sharon, you can have a thankful heart for a God who loves you, and who will take even terrible experiences like yours and turn them into an opportunity for good, as you go free in your own spirit, and then reach out and serve others with the same love that you have received from Him."

Sharon immediately perceived the truth of these things. Her peace and freedom of spirit were a vivid illustration of the results of allowing God to renew our minds (Romans 12:2). The renewing of our minds is *looking at ourselves and our circumstances from God's perspective* rather than from man's perspective, and that's exactly what Sharon did. With her circumstances and reactions in proper focus, we moved on to discuss how to deal with her uncles. "Sharon, you can't pretend that nothing ever happened," I said, "so my advice to you is to deal with it directly. You could approach each one and say, 'We both know what went on in the past. But I want you to know that Jesus Christ is now my Lord. He's forgiven me of *my* sins, He's provided for the forgiveness of *your* sins, and *I* forgive you, too.'

"Do any of your uncles know the Lord?" No, she said. I asked if she knew how to share the gospel, and again she said no. "I'll tell you what I'll do. We've written a little booklet that explains how to come to know Christ, and I'll send you one right away. It's very simple; all you have to do is read it with someone." Sharon was excited about the idea, and we concluded our phone conversation.

Three days later, Sharon called back. "Over the weekend," she said, "we had another family gathering, and the booklet you talked about didn't arrive in time. But I did as you suggested. I talked to each of my four uncles personally, and *I led two of them to the Lord!*"

What a miracle! A poor innocent child, abused in a degrading way, growing into a strong, compassionate, and clear-sighted young woman. She had every reason to hang on to self-pity, hatred, and bitterness for a lifetime, and the world would have encouraged her to do so. But instead she became preoccupied with the living Christ and, *controlled by His love,* she chose to respond to adversity in God's way. She could have viewed herself as a victim, but she chose instead to view herself as God sees her—His child, who has already received "everything [she needs] for life and godliness" (2 Peter 1:3). Sharon experienced a *changed* life because she experienced an *exchanged* life in Jesus Christ! Now she is free and helping other people to see and understand their freedom in Christ.

From the Old to the New

Sharon's life shows the power of the exchanged life. It is not enough to have glib answers to people's problems. Sometimes when we are without compassion, we become like vending machines. A person shares a personal heartache with us and, *pop*, out comes a Bible verse. Even biblical truth, such as "Give thanks in all circumstances," can be harmful when shared at the wrong time or in the wrong spirit—particularly when it is shared apart from a heart of compassion. In order to apply biblical *principles* for living, we must have the biblical *foundation* of understanding God's love and acceptance. Giving thanks in times of trouble makes no sense to us unless we are seeing ourselves and our lives from God's perspective.

It is also not enough to tell people what they should *stop doing*. How could Sharon, for example, simply let go of the very understandable emotions of bitterness, hatred, and self-pity? There is only one way: by developing a *totally new mind-set, a new preoccupation*. We are not able to let go of things until we have something new to hang on to.

It reminds me of a small child in a playpen, playing with his favorite teddy bear. Try to take that bear away, and you've got a real fight on your hands! After all, he loves that bear and is dependent on it. That bear provides comfort and fellowship, and it is an object to love. So how can you take that bear away without a commotion? It's simple: Get him a puppy. A puppy provides comfort and fellowship, and more. It is alive; not only can you love it, it can love you back. As the child becomes preoccupied with the puppy, he will forget all about the teddy bear, and you can remove it without his even noticing.

That's a simple illustration, but it reveals an important insight about human beings. The way to break a habit or preoccupation is by developing a *new* habit or preoccupation. The new will push out the old, just as light dispels darkness and truth dispels error. As the Bible says, "Rather, clothe yourselves with the Lord Jesus Christ, and do not think about how to gratify the desires of the flesh" (Romans 13:14). *He* is to be our primary concentration.

That's why the Bible continually says not only what *not* to do, but what *to* do. "Don't steal; instead, go to work." "Don't lie; instead, tell the truth." "Don't fight each other; instead, forgive, accept, and love one another." It's all summed up in Ephesians 4:22-24:

> You were taught, with regard to your former way of life, to
> put off your old self, which is being corrupted by its deceitful

desires; to be made new in the attitude of your minds; and to put on the new self, created to be like God in true righteousness and holiness.

Free to Serve in Love

I wish I had the space to tell a hundred more stories like Sharon's of how the message of God's grace powerfully changes lives, but that would take a whole library. They stand as proof that the truth really does set you free. People continue to argue and nitpick theological issues but, to use an old phrase, "The proof of the pudding is in the eating." The power of the undiluted gospel to transform lives is unexplainable by any natural means.

If there is a single principle that exemplifies the life of freedom under grace, to me it is Galatians 5:13: *"For you were called to freedom, brethren; only do not turn your freedom into an opportunity for the flesh, but through love serve one another"* (NASB). The Lord Jesus said in regard to His own life, "The Son of Man did not come to be served, but to serve, and to give His life as a ransom for many" (Matthew 20:28). He also said, "It is more blessed to give than to receive" (Acts 20:35). Paul added, "Do nothing out of selfish ambition or vain conceit, but in humility consider others better than yourselves" (Philippians 2:3).

The unmistakable sign that "Classic Christianity" is taking hold in a man's heart is when you see the beginnings of the same attitude that Christ had: "I am not here to be served, but to serve." There is nothing less natural to a human being than that attitude. Only the miracle of the gospel can produce it. How else can you explain the attitude and actions of someone like Sharon apart from the intervention of a miracle-working God?

❧

The title of this conclusion is a question: "Whatever Happened to the Real Thing?" The answer is, "Nothing." There is nothing at all wrong with the message! Neither is there anything *new* about the message of God's grace. When it is shared straight and undiluted, it transforms lives in the same dramatic way as it did in the early days after Pentecost. The problem is not with the message, it is with *us*. *We* have strayed away from the fullness of Christ into religion and legalism.

> Why is grace available only to the humble? Because only the humble will *receive* it. The humble will always find God to be gracious and compassionate.

The same sun that hardens clay also melts wax. In the same way, the message of God's grace hardens the heart of the proud and softens the heart of the humble. "God opposes the proud but gives grace to the humble" (James 4:6). Why is grace only available to the humble? Because only the humble will *receive* it. The humble will always find God to be gracious and compassionate. He will open the floodgates of His love to any man, woman, boy, or girl who comes to Him in humble faith. The Lord continues to say to you and to me:

> Here I am! I stand at the door and knock. If anyone hears My voice and opens the door, I will come in and eat with him, and he with Me (Revelation 3:20).

Listen, open the door of your heart, and discover that Classic Christianity is a Person—the living Lord Jesus Christ.

A PERSONAL INVITATION

If after reading *Classic Christianity* you realize that you have never accepted God's offer of salvation in Jesus Christ—or if you simply are *not sure* whether or not you are in Christ—I invite you to receive Him right now. John 1:12 says, "To all who received Him, to those who believed in His name, He gave the right to become children of God." In Christ is total forgiveness of sins, total acceptance, and eternal life.

Salvation is a free gift that you accept by faith. You are not saved by prayer, but prayer can be a way of concretely expressing your faith in Christ. For example, here is a suggested prayer:

> *Lord Jesus, I need You. Thank You for dying for the forgiveness of my sins and for offering me Your righteousness and resurrected life. I now accept by faith Your gift of salvation. Through Your Holy Spirit, teach me about Your love and grace, and about the new life that You have given me. Begin the work of making me into the person You want me to be. Amen.*

Again, there is nothing magical about praying these words. God is looking at the heart that trusts fully in Him.

If you have received Jesus Christ through reading *Classic Christianity* or if your life has been impacted in other ways through the ministry of this book, you may find out more through the website for this book, ClassicChristianity.com, or at my website, BobGeorge.net. May God bless you with a deep personal understanding and experience of His matchless love and grace!

You may reach us at **bobandamygeorge@yahoo.com.** You may also purchase my books and access many years of radio teaching programs at **BobGeorge.net.**

OTHER HARVEST HOUSE BOOKS
BY BOB GEORGE

Classic Christianity Study Guide
Life's Too Short to Miss the Real Thing

In the Christian life, a feeling of burnout or disappointment can often come from the attempt to live it in your own strength. How can you learn to rest in *God's* strength and find the freedom of his liberating love and grace? This study guide for *Classic Christianity* takes you deeper into every subject presented in the book. Scripture verses, questions, and relevant examples help you apply the Bible's truth and grasp who you are in Christ.

Growing in Grace with Study Guide
When Giving It All You've Got Still Isn't Enough

As a Christian, saved by grace and set free by grace, your next step is to *grow* in grace. This is all about keeping your eyes off yourself and on Jesus. About believing with utter certainty that He alone is able to complete His work in you.

If you find that you're being distracted by focusing on how well you're doing, how you look, and how much you're accomplishing, Bob George points you again to the truth of the Bible, urging you to rest in the care of your perfect Savior. *Growing in Grace* will help you freshly discover the joy of Jesus Christ living His life in and through you! *Includes helpful study guide for individual and small-group learning.*

Complete in Christ
Discovering God's View of You

Where do you find fulfillment in your life? In your relationship with God? Or has that been a disappointment to you? If you've come to see Christianity as irrelevant to "real life"—or perhaps just a route to self-improvement—you may be missing the path to true fulfillment. This exciting, practical resource will help you understand how your completeness in Christ is the foundation and source for a meaningful life.

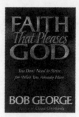

Faith That Pleases God
You Don't Need to Strive for What You Already Have

If you're like most Christians, you began your new life in Christ with joy and peace. But then, somehow your attempts to grow as a Christian—to please God—brought bewilderment, frustration, and defeat. You know there's a better way, but what is it?

Here, Bob George offers a practical look at true biblical faith—the kind of faith that produces the divine joy God offers to every believer. Learn why...

- true faith begins with the understanding that God is the initiator and we are responders to His grace.
- it's not the size of our faith that matters, but in whom we place our faith.
- we can't please God by continuing to ask Him for what He's already given us.

God wants every Christian to experience the abundant life—even during the hard times. The doorway to that abundance is labeled "faith"—faith that pleases God.

Victory over Depression
How to Live Above Your Circumstances

Depression. Hopelessness. Anger. Despondency. Sadness. These are some of the feelings you might experience when faced with difficult circumstances. But God has a bigger purpose for you than just getting rid of your problems. He wants you to *live above them.*

With a compassionate heart, Bob George shares how you can experience the reality of Jesus Christ as your hope in the midst of any seemingly hopeless situation. Whether poor relationships, past mistakes, personal tragedy, career or financial struggles, or illness, you can live above these circumstances by resting in the God who is far greater than any problem life can bring your way.

Other Harvest House Books to Help You Grow in Your Grasp of God's Love and Affection

Becoming Who God Intended
A New Picture for Your Past • A Healthy Way of Managing Your Emotions • A Fresh Perspective on Relationships
David Eckman

Whether you realize it or not, your imagination is filled with *pictures* of reality. The Bible indicates these pictures reveal your true "heart beliefs"—the beliefs that actually shape your everyday feelings and reactions.

David Eckman compassionately shows you how to allow God's Spirit to build new, *biblical* pictures in your heart and imagination. As you do this, you will be able to experience the life God the Father has always intended for you.

> "David Eckman is a man you can trust...
> His teaching resonates with God's wisdom and compassion."
> — STU WEBER,
> author of *Tender Warrior* and *Four Pillars of a Man's Heart*

Knowing the Heart of the Father
Four Experiences with God That Will Change Your Life
David Eckman

You're stuffed full of Christian information. But where is God in all of it? Perhaps Christianity seems irrelevant to where your heart is really at. Maybe you're thirsting for a *felt experience* of the Bible's truth. What if you could...

1. have an all-encompassing sense that you have a loving heavenly Dad?
2. have a sense of being enjoyed and delighted in by Him?
3. recognize that He sees you differently than you see yourself?
4. realize that *who you are* is more important to Him than *what you do?*

Do you want things to be different? See how these four great heart/soul transformations result in a vibrant, living faith that can stand up to the tests of life.

To learn more about Harvest House books and
to read sample chapters, log on to our website:

www.harvesthousepublishers.com

HARVEST HOUSE PUBLISHERS
EUGENE, OREGON